T0381462

BLOOD AND SHADOWS

MARK LEE

authorHOUSE

AuthorHouse™ UK
1663 Liberty Drive
Bloomington, IN 47403 USA
www.authorhouse.co.uk
Phone: UK TFN: 0800 0148641 (Toll Free inside the UK)
        UK Local: (02) 0369 56322 (+44 20 3695 6322 from outside the UK)

© 2025 Mark Lee. All rights reserved.

No part of this book may be reproduced, stored in a retrieval system, or
transmitted by any means without the written permission of the author.

Published by AuthorHouse 12/30/2024

ISBN: 979-8-8230-9122-0 (sc)
ISBN: 979-8-8230-9123-7 (e)

Library of Congress Control Number: 2024925972

Print information available on the last page.

Any people depicted in stock imagery provided by Getty Images are
models, and such images are being used for illustrative purposes only.
Certain stock imagery © Getty Images.

This book is printed on acid-free paper.

Because of the dynamic nature of the Internet, any web addresses or
links contained in this book may have changed since publication and
may no longer be valid. The views expressed in this work are solely those
of the author and do not necessarily reflect the views of the publisher,
and the publisher hereby disclaims any responsibility for them.

The life of

William Lee

Many thousands of men fought in the 2nd
World War, some were fortunate enough to have
survived. This is the true story of one of them,
many men followed the same battle path.
Like most he returned home with nothing but
memories in a time of continued hardship.
He built a family and taught them how to value
things, that family was everything, that having
very little was a blessing and these things along
with education was the key to a happy life.
This book is based on the memoires of my
father, the facts are as he wrote them.
I have written it in a fashion he would have
liked with more detail in some areas.
It will always be dedicated to him
and the family he made.

CONTENTS

CHAPTER 1

BORN OF DUST AND DREAMS

Summer is for Living not Learning

I FOLLOWED THE GANG ACROSS THE river, my feet skipping from one smooth stone to the next. The water swirled around my ankles, cold but not threatening—at least, not yet. Each stone was a test of balance, a challenge that made the crossing feel like part of the adventure, just another hurdle to get past before the real fun began. But then, in an instant, the ground disappeared beneath me. There was no warning, no time to react, only the sudden, shocking plunge into freezing water.

The cold hit me like a punch to the gut, forcing the breath from my lungs. It wrapped itself around me, pulling me down with relentless strength. I was seven years old, still a child, and had no understanding of death, not really. But in that moment, as the dark water closed over my head, I heard my mother's voice, clear and sharp, warning me—don't go near the river. Her words echoed in my mind, but they couldn't save me now. I was alone in the depths, sinking further into the blackness.

It got colder, the water pressing in on me from all sides, and I couldn't fight it. There was no way to fight it. My arms and legs were useless against the weight of the river, and I could do nothing but fall, helpless, deeper into that watery abyss. In those few terrible seconds, I knew fear for the first time—true fear. Not the childish dread of being caught or scolded, but something raw and primal. It was the kind of fear that seizes your soul, grips it tight and won't let go. It strips away every ounce of bravado, every thought, leaving only terror in its place.

This was not a fear I would forget. I had stepped into a place beyond the reach of daylight, a place where death lingered in the cold and the dark, waiting. It wouldn't be the last time I faced that kind of fear. I knew that even then, though I couldn't have put it into words. There was something about that descent, that plunge into the unknown, that marked me.

Time seemed to stretch on endlessly, my body no longer mine to command. I didn't struggle. The thought didn't even occur to me. And then, through the haze of cold and darkness, I felt it—something warm, something real. A hand, strong and sure, gripped my arm and pulled me upwards, hauling me out of the chasm.

It was Danny, my older brother, his face hard with determination as he dragged me into the light. The river released me, though not without a final, cold embrace. I gasped for breath, the world suddenly alive with warmth and sound. Danny had saved me, pulled me back from that dark place where fear lives. He dragged me to the riverbank, his face pale, his breath coming in harsh gasps as he laid me on the ground. The others stood by, wide-eyed and silent, watching as Danny knelt over me, waiting for signs of life. But I knew, even as I lay there on the riverbank, shivering and drenched, that I had glimpsed something I would carry with me forever. The river had let me go, but it had left its mark. And though I would face that same purgatory again, I knew I would never be the same as I had been before.

There were six of us, with Danny leading the charge, like always. He was the sort that never hesitated, not when there was something to be gained. This time, it was apples. The orchard by Cardiff Castle, tantalizing and forbidden, was ripe for the taking. The sun hung low in the evening sky, casting its warm, golden light across the land. The air was thick with the smell of smoke—someone burning something far off, the scent mingling with the dust and the heat. It was the kind of evening where the world felt alive, every sense heightened, the promise of adventure crackling in the air.

I could feel the dust on my skin, caked into my clothes after a long day of running wild, climbing trees, scaling walls, and dodging the kind of chores my mother insisted on. I hadn't washed, hadn't even thought about it—there were more important things to do. The dirt, the grime, it was the mark of a day well spent, a badge of honour. There was no time for the soap and water routine mothers always seemed to love, not when there were apples to be had.

We reached the river, the Taff, its waters flowing lazily, catching the last light of day in rippling flashes. I saw the gang stepping into the river, not hesitating, moving across it with confidence. My mind was already working, thinking of the best way to grab the most apples without getting caught. I could see the orchard in my mind's eye, the trees heavy with fruit, the sweet scent filling the air as we snuck through the branches. But I had to stay focused. I had to be faster, smarter than the others.

Danny and the rest were crossing the river by walking along an ancient Roman wall, sunken just beneath the water, a relic of the past, worn down by time but still sturdy enough to carry us. It ran alongside an old well, long forgotten, its mouth dark and ominous. I didn't know any of this at the time—didn't know about the wall, or the well. I was just following, as you do when you're young and full of fire, trusting the path without question, eyes set on the prize.

The water was cool, lapping at my legs as I stepped into the river. I kept my eyes on Danny's back, on the way his feet moved across the stones, and I followed. I had no idea of the history beneath me, of the silent dangers lying in wait. All I knew was the thrill of the chase, the taste of the apples almost on my tongue, and the certainty that, whatever happened, I'd find a way to come out ahead. That was the way of things. You didn't think too far ahead, not when you were that age. You just followed the leader, eyes on the horizon, ready for whatever came next.

He dragged me to the bank, his arms steady, unyielding, while the others stood at a distance, mute and uncertain. Dan was larger than life to me, towering in both stature and years, older by more than two and a half. In those days, there was no talk of resuscitation or life-saving breaths. We only knew the barest instinct of survival, the sharp bite of fear, and the cold indifference of fate.

For a moment, he knelt beside me, his breath ragged, his eyes searching my face for some sign of life. I sputtered, gasped, and that seemed enough. Without a word, he hoisted me onto his back. The weight of me, damp and limp, seemed to burden him not at all, though the journey ahead was far—two miles of winding paths, fields stretching lonely under the fading sky. The silence between us was thick with what had just passed, what might have been.

When at last we reached the house, I expected something—relief, perhaps even gratitude—but the air inside was colder than the water from which he had pulled me. My father's fury met us at the door, dark and immediate, like the coming of a storm.

"You should have watched him!" he shouted, his voice carrying an edge that cut through the room.

Dan, breathless still, shook his head in disbelief. "But I saved him," he murmured, the words catching in his throat. "He was drowning."

It didn't matter. My father's wrath was blind, unheeding. "If you had watched him, it would never have happened."

I stood there, a ghost in my own body, watching the scene unfold as though from a great distance, more astonished than Dan at the injustice of it. The tension hung in the air, bitter and unforgiving, and I knew then that something had shifted between us.

After that day, Dan kept his distance, as if by protecting me once, he had somehow marked himself. There was a wariness in his eyes whenever he saw me, a silent resolve not to let the weight of my presence pull him under again.

The house, the fields, even the very air we breathed seemed altered, as though a shadow had fallen over everything, darkening the edges of our lives.

I came into this world in 1922, in the heart of Cardiff, a city teeming with life and grit. Growing up as one of ten children, squeezed into a terraced house on Rodney Street, felt as natural as the rain that lashed against the windows or the coal smoke that thickened the air. It was a life of survival, of making do, and we knew no different. With husbands summoned to the front lines, our family, like countless others, was shaped and scarred by the crucible of the Great War. Five children had been born in those distant, more innocent days, before the world was ripped apart by the savage call of battle. Then came the war, casting a shadow over everything. But when at last the guns fell silent, when the blood had dried upon the fields of Europe and the wail of widows began to fade, five more of us followed.

Mary, the eldest, came into the world in 1908, and Sheila, the youngest, was born in 1924. For us younger ones, those firstborns seemed more like grown-ups than siblings — touched by an era we could barely comprehend, carrying the weight of a time before the storm that shattered families, and the world, forever. There were 6 girls and 4 boys, Mary born 1908, Helen (Cissy) 1909, Alice 1910, Margaret, 1911, John 1913, Tom 1919, Danny 1920, Elizabeth (Bette)1921, me 1922 and Sheila 1924.

Our house was cramped, just three bedrooms to fit a family that would have made others balk. My parents slept in the largest room, shared with my younger sister Sheila and my older sister Bette who were in a narrow single bed pressed up against the wall, while the rest of us made do as best we could. Tom, Dan, and I were packed into the second bedroom, like cargo lashed to a deck, close enough that we could feel each other's breath in the dark. John, my eldest brother stretched out in a single bed at the foot of ours, as though the space he occupied could contain the weight of all he was. It was no palace, but we were brothers, and there was a kind of comfort in the closeness, a strength that came from sharing space, even if it was small

The box room was where Alice and Margaret lay, crammed together in a single bed, and in some ways, it was a kingdom of their own. Privacy was a luxury we never even considered. We lived on top of each other, but it was the only way we knew how.

It was a strange way to grow up, perhaps, but in those days, it was as normal as the sun rising and the world turning.

Mary, my eldest sister, had her own escape. She lived with my grandmother just around the corner on Tredegar Street, and while it was only a short walk away, it felt like another world. She had found freedom there, of sorts, something the rest of us could only imagine.

And then there was my second eldest sister Cissy— Helen, as the others called her—but to us, she would always be Cissy. She had gone further still, to Swansea, to live with Aunt Liz and her husband, Mark. They had no children, and they took her in as if to fill a void, though what she found there, we could only guess.

There was no room for softness or sentiment in our lives. We fought for space, for food, for our place in the pecking order. It was a life of hard edges, of struggle and perseverance. But we were a family, and we faced it together, each of us learning, in our own way, to fight for what we needed. In those cramped rooms, where every breath felt shared, we grew strong. We had no choice.

There were about twenty terraced houses on our street, tightly packed, shoulder to shoulder like soldiers standing in line. Among them, some sixty children roamed—mostly teenagers, but a good mix of ages, all full of fire and life. In the summer, the street came alive. It was our kingdom, and every inch of it was claimed for games, laughter, and a fierce energy that seemed to rise with the heat of the sun.

Before the war came and changed everything, the seasons were as dependable as the tides. Summer didn't just arrive—it conquered. From June to September, the sun blazed in a sky so clear you'd swear it would never rain again. For four long months, it was heat and light, a golden time when the days stretched on forever, and the street was ours. We ran, we fought, we played. The air smelled of dust and sunshine, and nothing mattered except the thrill of each game and the strength of your companions.

But just as surely as the summer reigned, the other seasons came in their time, each one as predictable as the last. Autumn brought cooler air and leaves that crunched underfoot, while winter wrapped its icy fingers around us, testing our endurance. And spring—oh, spring—always came with its promise of new beginnings, a whisper of warmth that carried hope in its wake. April showers, March winds—each season knew its place and brought with it the feeling that life itself was renewing, repeating the joys we had known before.

We didn't have much—money was scarce, and luxuries were a distant dream—but we didn't care. The things that mattered couldn't be bought. It was the feeling of freedom as we ran down that narrow street, the camaraderie of boys and girls bound by the simple pleasures of life, the thrill of competition, and the satisfaction of belonging to something larger than yourself. These were the things that sustained us, the things that made those years feel rich and full despite the lack of wealth.

The world was changing, though. The war loomed on the horizon, and soon everything would be different. But back then, when the seasons obeyed the rhythm of time and we ruled our street, life felt like an endless adventure, and we never imagined how quickly it could all be swept away.

The summer school holidays were a time of unrestrained freedom, when the bonds of routine and responsibility were cast aside, and the world belonged to us. It was a season of exploration, when the rules of childhood were suspended, and reputations were forged in the heat of adventure. What happened in those long, sun-drenched days would be etched into our memories, becoming stories we'd retell on street corners for years to come. And as those stories were passed from one mouth to another, they grew, taking on the weight of legend.

To even consider schoolwork during that time was nothing short of sacrilege. Anyone caught with a book in hand or a pencil in their grip was marked as an outsider, and though we might offer a moment's pity, it was fleeting. We had little use for their kind. Schoolwork was an insult to the freedom we held dear, an invasion on the sacred ground of our summer, and we scorned it with every breath. That was the unspoken law: summer was for living, not learning.

In August, when the days were at their hottest, our gang—fifteen to twenty strong, sometimes more—would head for Sophia Gardens. There, the river Taff became our playground. It was in those waters that I first learned to swim. At five or six years old, I stayed in the shallows at first, the coolness of the river licking at my legs, but soon enough I ventured out with the older boys. The river had a way of calling you deeper, pulling you into its flow, until you found yourself swimming without fear, drawn by the sense of wildness that only water can give.

We made our own camps by the riverbank, using whatever we could find. Old sacks, once wrapped around sides of bacon, were discarded outside the warehouse, and we claimed them as our own. They stank, of course—the sharp smell of meat and salt—but we didn't care. We lashed them together with bits of string, and in our eyes, they became tents, as good as any real canvas. Those makeshift shelters gave us shade from the sun and a place to hide from the world.

We lived simply but well. Bread and jam sandwiches,

packed into paper bags, became our feast. We carried a flagon of water with us, but it wasn't long before we transformed it into something more. For a half penny's worth of sherbet, we mixed it into the water, turning it into our version of pop—a drink that fizzed and bubbled as we passed it around, laughing as we drank. It was all we needed to fuel our adventures for the day.

We roamed like conquerors, ruled by no one but ourselves, and each day was a battle won, another story to be told. Life was simple then, but it was full. And in those golden days of summer, with the sun on our backs and the river at our feet, we thought we had the world in our grasp. In a way, we did.

The canal that snaked through the heart of the city had long since passed its prime, yet it remained a favoured haunt for those bold enough to swim in its murky waters. Once a lifeline for the coal trade, this waterway had, in its heyday, borne the weight of barges heavy with black gold, ferrying the spoils from the distant mines in the valleys to the bustling docks. But now, it was a ghost of its former self, the surface thick with coal dust and the bodies of dead dogs, rats, and bloated, unidentifiable carcasses bobbing in the current like forgotten relics of a harsher time.

It was a wonder, looking back, that we didn't all come down with some foul disease. But that's the way of things—life teeters on the edge of ruin more often than we realize, and somehow, we carry on. From the old bridge at Kingsway, where the road hugged the side of the crumbling castle, passersby would toss ha'pennies into the canal for sport. Dan and his mates, lean and quick as jackals, would hurl themselves into the dark water, diving after the coins before they sank into the thick, grimy muck at the bottom. Once lost to the silt, no hand could retrieve them. It was a race against time, against the decay of the canal itself—a wild, reckless game, played in the shadow of a past that had long been swallowed by the blackened water

The barges lumbered along the canal, their hulking frames towed by the raw power of Shire horses, great beasts bred for their strength and endurance. Along the narrow towpath, which clung to the wall of the ancient castle on North Road, the horses plodded with a slow, steady rhythm. The walls of the castle loomed over them, a silent witness to centuries of change, though the canal had its own history, etched deep in the blackened water.

Halfway down the road, the canal met a lock gate. It was a place where the water was forced to bend to the will of man, where the barges paused as they were lowered to the next level of the canal, the operator staying aboard, his hands steady on the ropes. The cabin at the lock was a modest thing, though it had seen its share of the world—more than many men had, perhaps. Once through, the barges would drift past Kingsway Bridge, under the road, then slip like shadows beneath Queen Street, continuing their slow march towards the docks.

From Queen Street, the canal could be glimpsed through a tall, weathered wall, six feet high with a rusting metal gate embedded in it. That gate was no relic, though— it had purpose. It was for the Shire horses, allowing them to cross Queen Street and continue their work along Hills Terrace and Canal Street. The horses knew their path well, walking up the ramp to the gate, obedient to the rhythm of their lives. But the canal barge had no such luxury. Here, the bargees took matters into their own hands—literally. They would lie flat on the roof of the cabin, pushing the barge along by walking on top of the tunnel, until they reunited with the horse and resumed their journey on the Hills Terrace bank. There was no rest for these men. Their world was one of sweat, toil, and the unabated pull of necessity.

The horses would continue on towards Hayes Bridge, where the steps cut from the pavement led down to the canal bank itself. The bridge had seen its own share of life and death—of men and beasts both. We visited this place often. It was a part of the city's pulse, though the pulse could grow faint at times, drowned out by the whispers of tragedy. We all knew the stories, the warnings whispered by parents and elders, of children who had slipped into those dark waters and never returned. The canal could be merciless.

I remember one day with stark clarity. A priest, his face lined with sorrow, placed a single candle on a piece of wood and sent it drifting down the canal's gentle current. We watched, breath held, until the candle stopped, caught by the flow in a slow eddy. A diver was called, and it wasn't long before he pulled a small, lifeless body from the water. A boy, no more than seven or eight, claimed by the canal's dark depths.

But the canal wasn't all death and shadows. It could be kind too, in its own brutal way. My brother Tom was proof of that. He saved a boy from our street, dragging him from the cold water before it swallowed him whole. Tom wasn't one to speak of it, but I knew what he had done. He had faced the canal and won, at least that time.

The waterway ran on, towards the West Wharf, where the banks widened and the city seemed to let go of its past, if only for a while. On bright summer days, we would head there, our minds free from the gloom of the city, to swim in the canal's murky waters. The sun beat down on our backs, and for those brief hours, we felt invincible, untouched by the tragedies that swirled beneath the surface. Those were the days that linger, when the world seemed as endless as the canal itself.

We went to St David's School, tucked away in David Street, a place long since swallowed by the city's march towards progress. The Cardiff International Arena building stands where the old school once did, towering and indifferent to the memories it has buried beneath its foundations. But I remember that first day clearly, when my mother took me to start in the infants. The nuns ran the place—stern, disciplined women who ruled the school like a well-ordered ship. In the playground, the Sisters had set up a wooden table, and it was there, beneath the open sky, that they scribbled our names and addresses into a heavy ledger. It felt as though we were being conscripted into some grand undertaking, something bigger than we could yet understand.

Every morning, without fail, my mother would arrive at the entrance to the playground at morning breaktime. The clock would barely strike ten before she appeared, steady as the tide. In one hand, she'd carry a jug of tea, and in the other, a parcel of sandwiches wrapped in brown paper for me. A warm drink and food, to sustain me through till lunch, later, when my younger sister Sheila joined the infant's school, she would do the same for her also. No matter if the wind howled or the sun beat down relentlessly, she was there. Few mothers were as devoted. In a time where life could be hard, where comforts were few, my mother's love ran deeper than most, an anchor in the turbulent seas of our childhood.

But she wasn't alone in her morning vigil. There were three others—mothers who stood in silent solidarity, braving the weather and the long hours. Yet none had the same quiet determination, the same unwavering presence as my mother. She was always there, like clockwork, her love and devotion bound in every small act, every sip of tea, every bite of those simple sandwiches. She was a force, and though the world has moved on, though the school is long gone, the memory of her standing at the gate remains, as powerful as any warrior's march through history.

When I moved up to the boys' school, a new chapter began, one that was quite different from what I had known. The new building, towering and imposing, housed classrooms that seemed to stretch endlessly. Each room was packed with forty-five to fifty boys, a throng of youthful faces and restless energy squeezed into every available inch. It felt like being conscripted into a vast, unfeeling battalion, each of us a cog in the unstoppable machinery of education.

Winter came with its own brand of harshness. The cold was an unyielding adversary, creeping through the walls and settling deep into our bones. The classroom boasted only a single coal fire, its flickering warmth a scant comfort against the biting chill. We shivered in our seats, our breath visible in the icy air, but complaining was not an option. To voice our discomfort was to invite further hardship, and so we endured in stoic silence.

The teacher, a figure of authority and self-preservation, stationed himself next to the fire. His position was strategic, allowing him to rotate with the shifting heat, ensuring he was always within the fire's reach. His presence was a physical barrier, absorbing the warmth and leaving little for the rest of us. As he shifted from side to side, the warmth was unevenly distributed, a cruel jest played upon the students.

Those of us relegated to the back of the classroom bore the brunt of this arrangement. We were the coldest of all, sitting hunched and rigid, the chill seeping into our very bones. The fire's heat never reached us, leaving us in a perpetual state of discomfort, our attempts to warm ourselves fruitless. We sat there, enduring the cold and the silent resentment that came with it, our youthful resilience tested by the harsh conditions of our new schooling.

Our boots were heavy, laced with iron studs that bit into the earth as we walked. But not all of us had such fortune. Many went without, their soles worn thin by hardship. The Parish would step in sometimes, if a father was dead or too broken by the burden of unemployment to provide. You'd see boys, faces grim, handed a pair of rough boots—new to them, but worn by others before, leather cracked and patched. Those without such charity made do. Some would nail old tyre tread to the bottoms of their boots, the rubber giving just enough life to carry them through another day. Others wore clogs, wooden, unyielding, clattering through the streets with each step. We didn't complain. We couldn't afford to. In those days, money was as scarce as hope, and we made do with what we had.

In the biting cold of winter, I'd race home from school, barely two streets away, the sharp wind stinging my cheeks. As I entered the passageway of our house, I was greeted by the rich, comforting aroma of my mother's soup—there was nothing like it in the world. It was simple, hearty, and always delicious. I could never get enough, my appetite as big as my hunger for life itself.

My father, a man of grit and principle, was a master of the noble art of boxing. Bare-fisted, he fought many men in our area, though never by choice—only when pushed to it, and always came out the victor. In the backyard, he'd built a boxing ring with his own hands, just for me, Dan, and Tom. He wanted us to be strong, to know how to defend ourselves in a world that wouldn't always be kind. He'd even set up a pear-shaped punch ball for us to train on, hammering away at it, building our arms and our spirit with each strike.

Those were hard days, but they were ours, and they shaped us into men.

Every day without fail, he worked that punch ball, his fists a blur of precision and rhythm. He could keep a steady beat for what seemed like hours, the dull thud of leather against leather filling the air like the rhythm of a drummer's call to battle. It wasn't just exercise—it was a ritual, a way to heal what had once been broken. His right elbow had taken the worst of it, a lasting injury from his time in France. Dad had been in the infantry, in the First World War, The Welsh Regiment—same as I would join in time to come. In Mametz Woods, he and two mates were caught in the blast of a mortar shell, buried alive for two days beneath the cold earth. By some miracle, they were dug out, but the damage was done. He spent months in a hospital bed in France, mending slowly.

After that, his right arm was never the same, but he refused to let it wither. He used that punch ball to keep it alive, working the joint with fierce determination. The rhythm of his strikes became so regular, it was like listening to a tap dancer, each punch perfectly timed, perfectly placed. He loved it—the power, the control. It was as if with each hit, he was beating back the past, refusing to let those dark days of war claim any more of him than they already had.

I remember a story, told many times, from when my father was courting my mother. They were walking together, arm in arm, towards her house one evening, when they spotted her father standing on the doorstep. He was a quiet, unassuming man, not the sort to invite trouble, but that night trouble had found him. O'Leary, the Irish bully and braggart of the neighbourhood, was standing there tormenting him, sneering, hurling insults at my grandfather as though he were beneath contempt.

My father saw the scene unfolding as they approached, his eyes sharpening, but his pace never quickened. He walked with a calm, unshakable confidence, a man who had faced fear and mastered it long ago. O'Leary, in a fit of drunken rage, was screaming obscenities, his voice echoing down the cobbled street, but none of it reached my father. He didn't need words—there was nothing to be said.

When they finally stood face to face, close enough for O'Leary to take the first shot, my father stood tall, watching the man's eyes. He had learned long ago that you could read a man's intentions in the flicker of his gaze, the twitch of his body. And the moment O'Leary made his move, my father was ready. In the blink of an eye, he blocked the clumsy strike and delivered three rapid-fire punches—one to the ribs, another to the jaw, and a final blow that sent O'Leary stumbling back.

The street was long and cobbled, and with the same unbreakable rhythm my father had honed on the punch bag for years, he sent O'Leary reeling from one end to the other. Each punch landed with the precision of a craftsman at work.

It wasn't out of rage, but out of discipline—a rhythm of power and control that only years of hard practice could perfect.

When my father decided O'Leary had had enough, the bully was a broken man, gasping for air. He didn't leave it there, though. O'Leary was made to stand, to face my grandfather, and apologise for his insults, his pride stripped bare. From that day forward, the braggart showed respect to the old man, and the legend of my father's quiet, unshakable strength spread through the streets. It wasn't just his fists that taught the lesson—it was the way he carried himself, with dignity, and a fearlessness that could not be matched.

My Dad was a resourceful man. We didn't have much, and when we couldn't afford things, he would find a way to make them himself. We thought the world of him for it. The area we lived in was no different from anywhere else in those days—nobody had much, and certainly no one was well-off. A wireless was a rare luxury, and even then, only if it was rented. But what every street had, without fail, was a pub. Only men were allowed inside, of course. Women could go into the snug—a tiny little room tucked away to the side, just big enough for four people, if that.

Most Saturday nights, us kids would be tucked up in bed, but we knew the real entertainment was yet to come. We'd lie there, ears pricked, waiting for the inevitable sounds of a fight to break out in the street. It wasn't long before we'd hear the shouts and scuffling, and we'd scramble to open the windows, peering out for a grand view of the action below. That was until my mother caught wind of what we were up to. She'd be up those stairs in no time, closing the windows and warning us not to open them again—but of course, we always did.

My father never showed himself up in those street brawls. He wasn't one for drunken quarrels. He was a quiet, intelligent man, more concerned about our development than his own pride. He believed in strength and discipline, not just of the body but of the mind. To help build that strength, he even put up a pair of rings in the backyard, and I'd pull myself up on them every day. That made me strong, extra strong, and Dad was always pleased with my progress.

He had dreams for us, especially when it came to boxing. He put the big gloves on me and Dan, made us spar against each other in the backyard. But it didn't last long. My mother didn't like it one bit. She raised hell about it, complaining that we'd hurt ourselves, and eventually, Dad stopped making us spar. It was a pity, really. He had always hoped one of us would take up boxing, follow in his footsteps, but after he died, my mother made sure of it—she even went so far as to burn the gloves.

Had he lived, I've no doubt me and Dan would've ended up in some kind of sport. Maybe not boxing, but gymnastics or something that would've made use of the strength Dad had helped us build. Still, I carry his lessons with me, and in a way, that's more than enough.

My brother John couldn't find a job, so at just 17, he up and joined the Welsh Guards stationed in London. He didn't tell anyone, just left. My mother was beside herself when she found out, heartbroken. To her, he was still a boy, and London felt a world away. But John was desperate to make something of himself, and in those days, the Guards seemed like a chance for a future, even if it came at a price.

Meanwhile, my father was struggling. He was a Docker, unloading cargo down at the docks, but work was scarce. He wasn't employed regularly, only when there was an urgent need, when a ship had to be unloaded fast. Hundreds of Dockers stood about waiting for their chance to work, like wolves circling a carcass, hoping for a scrap. Some days it came, most days it didn't.

I remember one evening he came home, his face and clothes covered in a thick layer of red dust, the iron ore he'd been unloading clinging to his skin like blood. His head was bandaged, and I'll never forget the way My mother's face paled when she saw him. The hook of the crane had swung wild and hit him hard. He'd been to Cardiff Royal Infirmary, but they didn't do much for him. They just bandaged his head, dressed the wound, and sent him on his way, as if it were just another cut and bruise. But that blow to the head, that innocent-looking injury, would grow into something far more deadly—a tumour that would take his life in later years.

He knew none of that, of course. The next day, despite the bandage, despite the pain, he went right back to the docks. There was no choice. If he didn't work, there was no money, and if there was no money, there was no food on the table. Sickness, injury—it didn't matter. In those days, a man couldn't afford to stay home. The crane driver had been at fault, but there was no justice for the working man. No sickness benefit, no compensation. You got hurt, you got up and carried on, because no one else would carry it for you. That was the way of things back then. It was hard, but it was life, and we lived it the only way we knew how—by surviving.

My mother was a hard-working, loving woman, though when you're young, you take it all for granted. It's only when you grow older that you begin to see the sacrifices she made, the weight she carried just to keep us all going. To survive, she even turned our front room into a small shop. She sold sweets, groceries, vegetables, and sticks for kindling. She'd spend hours making toffee apples just to scrape together enough money to keep food on the table, because Dad's work at the docks was never guaranteed.

Every morning, without fail, he'd be up at 5:30 a.m., walking down to the docks, hoping for a day's work. But most days, he came back empty-handed. The ships weren't always in, and the competition was fierce—hundreds of men, all desperate for the same few hours of labour. On those rare days when he got the call, we'd have a bit more to eat, a bit more hope, but more often than not, we were left to rely on my mother's grit and determination.

She did what she could, but the weight of it all was endless. Many of the neighbours would buy from her shop on credit, promising to pay her back when they had the money. But times were hard all around, and soon my mother was owed so much she had no choice but to shut the shop. There was no bitterness in her, though. She did what she had to, always with love and without complaint, even as the burden grew heavier. It's only now, looking back, that I truly understand the depth of her strength, the quiet sacrifices she made so that we could survive.

During the Great War of 1914-1918, while Dad was away in France, fighting in the trenches like millions of other men, my mother was left behind to feed and clothe the five children she had at that time. It was a time of hardship, when survival came down to grit and endurance. Every morning, often as early as five o'clock, she would make her way to Edward England's Potato Wharf in the West Dock. The work was brutal. She'd push a heavy sack truck loaded with two one-hundredweight sacks of potatoes, hauling it from Tindel Street Wharf all the way up the steep incline of Bute Road, past the city, to the potato warehouse on the Hayes.

In those days, lorries couldn't be used. The war had drained the country of petrol, so everything had to be done by hand. The labour was backbreaking, yet my mother never hesitated. After three long hours of pushing, hauling, and unloading, she'd return home, exhausted but determined, to get the children fed, dressed, and ready for school.

Life was merciless back then. People didn't have the safety nets or government aid we see today. There was no help to catch you when times got tough. People could and did starve. And yet, my mother kept going, day after day, driven by a love so strong it defied the hardship. She endured the impossible, not for herself, but for her family. Those were the sacrifices that held our family together, though as children, we were too young to understand the weight of it. It's only now, looking back, that I realize just how hard life was for her, and how much we owe her for the quiet strength she carried in her every step.

I recall the scene with a clarity that haunts me still: my father, borne down the narrow staircase on a stretcher, a sight so stark it has never faded from my memory. The ambulance, with its stolid and sombre presence, was destined for Chepstow Military Hospital, and with it went our last glimpse of him.

On the morning that followed his death, the day was shrouded in a quiet, oppressive stillness. We were dressing for school, the usual routine punctuated by an unexpected and jarring knock echoed through the house. The sound was sharp, authoritative—a policeman's knock. My mother's face turned ashen as she ushered him into the front room, her movements stiff and mechanical.

The policeman's presence seemed to deepen the silence, his words cutting through it with a brutal finality. He delivered the news we already feared: Dad had passed away in the night, February 16th, 1932, I was 9 years old and left in the cold grip of his absence. The utterance of those words seemed to rip the very ground from beneath us. My mother's reaction was one of sheer, unbridled anguish. She screamed, a cry that seemed to rend the air itself, and then she collapsed, her body crumpling into the nearest chair. Her sobs, raw and unrestrained, filled the room, and we—all of us—joined her in our grief, our tears blending with hers in a collective mourning. That morning is etched in my memory with a clarity that remains both vivid and painful.

The policeman, with a solemnity that felt almost cruel, turned to Tom and said, "You're the man of the house now." The gravity of his words hung heavily in the room. Though John was older, he was stationed in London with the army, and so it was Tom who, despite his youth, was thrust into a role that seemed far beyond his years.

The funeral remains etched in my mind like an impression in wax. In those days, a hearse was no mere vehicle—it was a stately procession, drawn by four black horses, each adorned with ostrich feathers, the plumes held in place by black bands encircling their foreheads. Behind this solemn conveyance came a small, enclosed carriage, its sombre interior designed for a select few, drawn by a single horse. We, the children, followed at a distance, a line of mourners moving slowly through the streets of Hayes and Kingsway, until we reached Cathays Cemetery. For us, that journey felt interminable, a landscape of sorrow stretching endlessly before us.

Everyone was cloaked in black, a sea of mourning that swept through the streets. In those days, the weight of grief was tangible, often forcing families into debt to afford the proper mourning attire. Men, too, would take the day off work in a gesture of respect—a far cry from the brief, perfunctory absences of today. A day's pay was a significant sacrifice, but it was expected, a mark of honour and duty that could not be disregarded.

Father was but 51 when he left us. My mother, left behind, was unable to claim any recompense for the accident at work that had led to the tumour that eventually claimed his life. The legal labyrinth demanded funds for a solicitor, funds she did not possess. It was a harsh reality, one that cast a shadow over our lives, a sharp reminder of the precariousness of our existence and the indifference of a world that offered no solace.

My Mother

I had a bike—or at least, what I convinced myself was a bike. It was a creation born not from luxury but from necessity, a product of my own hands, pieced together with a kind of wild determination. The frame was from an old man's bicycle, a relic salvaged from somewhere, and I had attached small, round pram wheels in place of proper ones. There was no seat, just a piece of old sacking rolled and tied, making it barely functional, but to me, it was everything. There was no chain either, so I had to run alongside it, gathering speed before leaping onto the contraption, balancing with a grace learned only through trial and error. I could see the eyes of the boys on our street—some filled with envy, others with awe—as I passed them by. Their silent admiration made the ungainly bike feel like the finest machine ever made.

And then, there was the hoop—a simple, rusted bicycle wheel, stripped of its spokes, yet it held the charm of something rare. We'd run alongside it, sticks in hand, tapping it with a steady rhythm to keep it rolling over the uneven cobbles. But those who were truly fortunate had something more—a car tyre. Bigger, heavier, more substantial than any hoop, it was the treasure of our games. To own a car tyre was to be crowned king of the street, and those who had one ruled with an unspoken authority. The rest of us would chase after it, our hearts pounding with desire.

Those summers, when we ran wild with daps on our feet and makeshift toys in our hands, were a time untainted by the weight of the world. They were raw, simple, yet overflowing with life's purest joys. Those fleeting days of freedom lingered long in the memory, a reminder of a world that was once entirely ours.

Another vehicle I built was a bogey, a marvel of makeshift engineering that only a boy with ambition and a handful of scrap could dream up. It started with a solid plank of wood, sturdy enough to carry a boy and the dreams of speed, yet light enough to move freely down the hill. Four pram wheels, salvaged from the back alleys, served as the foundation, their metal axles attached with whatever bolts and nails I could find.

The genius of it, though, lay in the front axle. I made sure it could pivot either way—left or right—to steer the bogey as it barrelled down the street. A simple wooden pole was the key to its motion, gripped firmly in hand, pushing the contraption along as I sat on the open box that served as a seat. The faster you pushed, the faster you flew, and the thrill of it was unmatched.

The other kids would line up just for the chance to push you along, racing each other to claim their turn. There was a hierarchy in the street, and for those precious minutes, as the bogey careened forward, you were king. The laughter, the cheering—it all blended into a symphony of youthful exuberance, and as long as the wheels held steady, nothing in the world could touch you.

Christmas was a time of joy and wonder, though not for the abundance of toys, but for something far deeper. We may have had only two toys, but my mother always made sure our stockings were filled with oranges, apples, and nuts. It was that happy, close-knit family feeling that made the season marvellous. There was a warmth in our little house that no amount of riches could buy.

Us children would try to save up what little we had—halfpennies, slowly adding up to one shilling by Christmas. That shilling was our treasure, meant for sweets. We'd go to Chapple's, the sweet shop, we'd get ten assorted little bags of sweets for half a penny each. Each bag was a different delight, carefully packed into a shoebox, which we'd take home and place on top of my mother's wardrobe, waiting for Christmas Day to come.

Dinner was a feast, and somehow, every year, my mother would manage to put a goose on the table. In those days, a goose was the top bird, long before turkeys came over from America. We were fortunate, because some families down our street would have nothing more than a rabbit, or worse, no Christmas dinner at all. But no matter what was on the table, the day was filled with laughter and a deep sense of belonging.

Maybe once, we'd go to the pantomime, that grand spectacle where the magic of the season came alive before our eyes. And no one sent Christmas cards—not like today. It simply wasn't done in our street. We didn't need them; our family's love and presence were enough.

We were never rich in money, but we were rich in the things that truly mattered. We always had enough to eat, and my mother made sure we were dressed well. For all the simplicity of those days, Christmas was a time of love, warmth, and family, things that last longer than any gift ever could.

When I think back, it strikes me how things were in those days. Boys didn't wear long trousers until they'd left school and entered the world of work. Until that day, we braved every season, even the bitter winters, in short trousers. The wind would cut through the fabric, biting at our legs, but it was the way of things, and we accepted it without complaint. We had no choice, after all.

The other item we all wore was a jersey. It was as much a part of a boy's uniform as the trousers themselves. I remember some of the boys wearing their jerseys until they were threadbare, full of holes, practically disintegrating on their backs. But there was little concern for fashion or new clothes. You made do with what you had, and when that jersey finally gave way, only then might you get another. They weren't wool, either—nothing as warm or durable. They were made of some kind of rough nylon, itchy against the skin, but it was what we had.

Those days were hard, but we didn't think much of it at the time. It was just life, and we faced it head-on, as boys do, with little thought for the cold or the wear of a jersey hanging by its last thread.

Sheila was a creature of the water, graceful and swift, a natural talent that seemed as though it had been gifted to her by the very sea. I can still picture her, part of St David's School Swimming Champions team, her dark hair slicked back, her eyes filled with quiet determination. There was one evening in particular, a night that remains etched in my memory, when her prowess in the water brought her school—our school—unparalleled glory.

It was the annual Gala, where the Catholic schools of Cardiff gathered to compete, to discover which team would claim the title of the best. Guildford Crescent swimming baths, the only pool in those days, was filled with the sound of cheers and splashing water. Outside, under the summer sky, hundreds of schoolchildren stood in a fever of anticipation. We crowded the streets, our hearts racing with every announcement, every whisper of which team had excelled in the race.

At last, the doors of the baths swung open, and an official stepped forward. "St David's has won the Gala!" he declared, and in that instant, the night became a whirlwind of celebration. We erupted into cheers, our voices rising high into the warm evening air. We waited eagerly for the champions to emerge, our eyes fixed on the doors. When Sheila and her teammates finally appeared, they were carried like heroes on the shoulders of the boys, their victory immortalized in that jubilant parade up David Street, past the convent and toward St David's Church Hall, where the Arena stands today.

The Rose Bowl, glinting in the fading sunlight, was theirs. But that wasn't all. Sheila had outdone herself, winning not only for the team but taking home a silver medal and two bronze ones of her own. The Sisters greeted the champions with open arms, their pride palpable as they praised the triumph of St David's. And we, delirious with joy, sang our school song as loudly as our voices would allow—"Who said St David's couldn't win, St David's couldn't win at all," a chant that seemed to echo long into the night. Sheila, I am certain, would remember that evening as vividly as I do.

Yet, time is a strange and often cruel thing. What had once been the height of her success, her life filled with the promise of further victories, soon turned to dust. Sheila's knee began to trouble her, a nagging pain that worsened as the years passed. The doctors—men we trusted with our very lives—insisted her leg be set in plaster, held rigid to heal. It was meant to help, but instead, it became her undoing. The plaster, left for too long, locked her joints in place, making it impossible for her to bend her knee again.

It was during this time that I was abroad fighting in the war, gone for three and a half years, unaware of what was happening at home. When I finally returned on leave, I was horrified to see her leg encased in that infernal plaster. I was furious—how could they have allowed this to go on? How could they not see the damage they were causing? But by then, the time for anger had passed. The harm had already been done, and there was no going back.

Sheila, once the brightest star in the water, would never swim the same way again. The doctors—those ignorant, well-meaning fools—had taken that from her. And though years have passed, the memory of what might have been, of what was so unfairly lost, still lingers like a shadow over those long-ago summer nights.

This was a time well before the benefits of the National Health Service, in fact in those days, no one even had the luxury of an indoor toilet. Every house on our street had theirs outside, standing at the far end of the garden. I remember the walk from the back door, through the garden, maybe thirty-five feet or so to the small brick structure that housed the toilet. It was a journey you thought twice about in the dead of winter, especially at night, but it was all we knew.

Right next to the toilet was the wash house, a small, smoke-blackened building where my mother performed the weekly ritual of laundry. Every Monday without fail, she'd be out there, boiling up the family's clothes. She had an old iron drum, heavy and cast like an upside-down dome, built into the ground with a fire lit underneath it. The flames would crackle and roar, turning the water into a rolling boil. One by one, she'd lower the clothes into the cauldron, starting with the whites, letting them churn in the bubbling water until they were clean.

There was no respite, no help offered. My mother was a one-woman machine. After the boiling was done, the wet clothes were hauled out and passed through the mangle, a massive wooden roller designed to squeeze out every drop of water. She'd turn that handle, her hands red and raw from the cold and the work, until each piece of clothing was pressed dry enough to be hung. No one came to help her. It was her burden alone, week after week, but she did it without a word of complaint, as if it were simply the way things had to be.

Looking back, I marvel at her strength. That wash house was her battlefield, and each Monday she fought her way through it with a quiet determination, never asking for thanks or assistance. It was just another day in a life where no task was ever too small or too hard to do alone.

In the dead of winter, we always held out as long as we could before facing the ordeal of going to the toilet in the dark. The cold was a biting thing, relentless, seeping into your bones, and we dreaded the journey outside. There was no avoiding it—when nature called, you had to go. We'd take a candle with us, a fragile flame flickering in the bitter wind, but more often than not, the gusts would find their way in, snuffing it out in a matter of seconds. The night, wild and unforgiving, always seemed to have the upper hand.

You'd ask someone to come along, hoping for company, for a little comfort in the darkness, but no one would agree. Everyone knew the trek was something you faced alone. Except for my mother. She had a kind heart, and sometimes, if you pleaded long enough, she'd come with you. She'd stay close, walking with you to the toilet, her presence like a shield against the shadows. But as soon as you were inside, she'd leave, heading back to the warmth of the house, leaving you to face the cold.

Inside the toilet, the air was frigid, your breath hanging

in the small space like a mist. There was no time to linger—you rushed through the business as fast as you could, the cold biting at your skin, and then you ran, legs pumping, back to the house. The cold didn't care for haste. Many times, you'd return with wet legs, the hurried movements only making matters worse, but at least you were back in the warmth. The house never felt so welcoming as it did then, with the wind howling outside, battering the walls, and the darkness held at bay.

We had no electricity in those days. The candle was our lifeline, the one source of light in the thick black of the night. Especially when we went to bed, its weak glow was the only thing between us and the shadows. It wasn't much, but it was all we had, and we made do.

Then the day came when electricity was installed. I remember it well. It was nothing short of a miracle. To press a switch and have light flood the room—it was like something from a different world. The dark corners that had once seemed so full of menace were banished in an instant. There was no more battling the wind with a trembling candle. No more wet legs from rushing back in the freezing night. The electric light changed everything. But still, those nights in the winter, facing the cold and the dark, remained etched in my mind—a reminder of a harder, wilder time.

With or without electricity my mother had to be a master at managing the little we had, and she would save for months through Lermons Savings, just to ensure we had proper clothes for Corpus Christi. It wasn't just for me but for Tom, Dan, Bet, and Sheila too. Back then, you didn't just walk into a shop, take what you needed, and promise to pay later. No, everything had to be paid for in full before it left the shop. That meant each week, without fail, my mother would put a little aside, making sure we had enough when the time came to buy what we required.

Lermons was the place to go, a big drapery stall on Hayes Bridge Road. It was well-known in our area, especially among the Catholic families. They stocked everything for Corpus Christi—suits and shoes for the boys, white dresses and veils for the girls. And because everyone in our community knew the importance of that day, Lermons did a brisk trade. You could see mothers like mine, week after week, handing over what little they had, determined to have their children properly dressed for the occasion.

There was no such thing as "buy now, pay later" like there is today. It simply wasn't possible in those days. In truth, it was probably for the best. Once people had the clothes in hand, there would've been no spare money left to pay off debts. There was barely enough to get by as it was. My mother knew that well, and she managed to stretch every penny, not because it was easy, but because it was necessary.

Our Bet was the one who always went to the shops for my mother or Auntie Jule. She had a way about her, a steadfastness, as if she carried the weight of the household on her young shoulders. She never forgot a thing, always knowing just what to buy. I would watch her from the doorway as she ran up Tredegar Street, her heels kicking up behind her as though they were in a race with the wind. She was quick, reliable, and even at the age of 8yrs old there was something almost serene in her competence.

Auntie Jule lived just across from us, and every Monday, without fail, she'd send one of us to Sollies, the pawn shop down on Bute Terrace. I can still remember the sight of those woollen blankets in our arms, soft and threadbare, carried to the pawn shop like a ritual, exchanged for a few coins to tide Auntie Jule over until Friday, when her sons' wages would come. The blankets would come home again by the week's end, retrieved with the pawn ticket and a few pence more than we'd left with. It was a small price to pay, Auntie Jule would say, for a little help when you needed it most.

But my mother hated it, hated the thought of her children being seen going in and out of the pawn shop. It weighed on her, though she never said a word against Auntie Jule. It wasn't in her nature to cause a stir. Still, I could see the quiet sorrow in her eyes whenever one of us set off to Sollies, her lips pressed into a thin line. My mother never pawned anything herself, not even when times were hard. It wasn't pride, not exactly—it was something deeper, something quiet and resolute.

Auntie Jule had other errands for us too, ones that my mother disliked just as much. On occasion, she'd send me or Dan to the Bridgewater pub to fetch two flagons of bitter beer. We'd carry them back carefully, their dark liquid sloshing against the sides of the jug. My mother, always so gentle, would never say anything about it. She would watch us go with a silent disapproval, a quiet unease that spoke louder than any words could. She was a woman who bore her worries with grace, a soft-spoken strength that wrapped itself around our little home like a blanket against the world.

There was something tragic in it all, in the small, everyday sacrifices we made, the quiet dignity with which my mother held herself, and the way we children played our parts in the rhythm of life without fully understanding its weight.

Born out of hardship there was the odd highlight, our Tommy was fortunate enough to have a bike, and it wasn't by chance either. My mother had gotten it through the new scheme Halfords had introduced, where you could buy a bike on credit, paying a steady 2/6d each week. But there was a catch—miss even one payment, and they'd come to reclaim it without a second thought. My mother wouldn't let that happen, not for Tom. He needed that bike to get to work at Robinson and David's timber merchants down on East Moors Road. It was more than just a convenience; it was his livelihood.

That bike became his prized possession, gleaming under his constant care. He'd spend hours polishing the frame, ensuring every part was spotless. None of us were allowed to touch it, not even to move it from its place against the wall. The mere suggestion would earn you a dark look from Tom. It was his pride, his mark of independence, and he guarded it fiercely.

Tommy was the only one among us who had a money box too, a small tin contraption with a rattling lid. He'd drop pennies and halfpennies into it, counting and recounting the coins as if his future were hidden in the clink of the metal. Dan, on the other hand, couldn't resist temptation. Every now and again, he'd slip a hand into the box and steal a halfpenny, thinking Tommy wouldn't notice. But Tom always knew. He had an uncanny knack for keeping track, as if each coin had its own place in his mind. And when he found out, he'd make Dan give it back, not in anger but with a quiet, stern insistence that left no room for argument.

It wasn't just about the money or the bike; it was about something more. For Tommy, that bike and those pennies represented a kind of control, a way to carve out something that was his alone in a world where very little came easily.

CHAPTER 2

SHADOWS OF YOUTH

**The tumult of teenage years—when
rebellion stirs and destinies start to form.**

I LEFT SCHOOL AT THE START of the Christmas holidays
in 1936, my childhood slipping away as the cold winds
of December swept through the streets. I was eager to find
work, to step into the world of men, and it wasn't long before
I saw the notice—a job advertised on a board outside a
building in Charles Street. Carter's Printing Works, it read,
and without hesitation, I walked inside, feeling both excited
and uncertain. By Monday morning, I was there, ready to
work, though I could never have imagined how quickly I'd
tire of the place.

The job itself was simple, though it demanded more
strength than I had thought. I was tasked with sweeping up
the scraps of paper that gathered at the foot of the cutting
machines, fine slivers that flew through the air like snow

and landed in untidy heaps on the floor. With each sweep, I filled a great sack, and then came the hardest part—pulling down a lever with both hands, summoning every bit of strength I had. The lever compressed the paper into what they called a bail and it was then tied tight with wire.

There was a great handcart in the yard, old and heavy, the sort of thing that seemed to have been part of the place for centuries. It would be piled high with packets of typing paper, and it fell to me to push it, the weight of it bearing down on me as I struggled to guide it through the streets. I remember the journey well, pushing that cart all the way down to the bottom of Cathedral Road. More often than not, the damned thing would tip over, spilling paper everywhere, and I'd have to gather it up again, my arms aching from the effort, while passersby either laughed or turned away.

By the time Friday arrived, I had reached my limit. The monotony of the work, the weight of the cart, the endless sweeping—it had drained every ounce of energy from me. When I collected my pay for the week, seven shillings, in today's decimal currency it would amount to thirty-five pence, I knew it was time to go. I left Carter's that evening, not looking back, knowing in my heart that I was meant for something more than sweeping paper scraps off a factory floor.

My next job was with the Swift Parcel Delivery Service, and for the first time, I felt a sense of freedom in my work. Often, I would find myself travelling all over the valleys, through winding roads that stretched into the hills. There was something about the job that suited me, something about the small, close-knit nature of the firm. I remember most clearly the car we used—an open-top Sunbeam, sleek and powerful, its engine humming beneath me as if it were alive. It was a beautiful car, one that turned heads as it sped through the narrow streets and country lanes, the wind whipping through my hair as my boss drove.

My boss had to use a car, as he couldn't secure a licence for vans to carry parcels. The railway people objected, fearful that his business might threaten theirs, and so the ambition of expanding beyond those few parcels was always just out of reach. It kept us small, kept us humble. But I didn't mind—I enjoyed the work, the freedom of being on the road.

Eventually, I was transferred to the valleys paper delivery run as a van boy, which was a far harder business. My days began in darkness, at three o'clock in the morning, when the world was still silent and cold. I would load the van with bundles of newspapers and parcels, each weighing a hundredweight, and set off into the Rhondda Valleys, delivering the morning's news to the shops that dotted the winding roads. It was a hard, endless job, made worse in the winter, when snow piled up in thick drifts along the roads, threatening to trap us as we made our way through the frozen landscape. We wouldn't return to the depot until five in the evening, our bodies weary from the long hours, the cold biting through to our bones. And for all this, eight shillings a week—hardly enough to make ends meet, but it was work, and I was glad of it.

I stayed on for a year, though it wasn't long before I found myself on the horse-drawn vans, collecting parcels from warehouses in the heart of Cardiff for delivery beyond the city. There was something about the rhythm of it that

I loved—the steady pace of the horses, the clatter of their hooves on the cobbles, the way the city came alive in the early hours as the sun began to rise. I took pride in the work, until the firm was bought out, first by Pickfords, and then by the railway. The business changed, lost the charm it once had, and though I stayed for as long as I could, it was never quite the same. The independence I'd once known had been swallowed by something larger, something more impersonal, and with it, a part of me longed for the open roads once again.

My next job was at Marks and Spencer, a far cry from the open roads of the valleys and the clatter of horse-drawn vans. I worked as a stockroom man, a role that seemed, at first glance, mundane but offered its own peculiar rhythm. Each day, I moved through the store's corridors like a ghost behind the scenes, unseen by the shoppers who filled the aisles below. My task was simple: to transport clothes— shirts, underwear, and all manner of garments— from the stockroom to the counters where they would be neatly arranged for sale. The stockroom itself was perched high on the top floor, and I would often find myself loading up the four-wheeled basket skip, filled to the brim with the day's goods, and then guiding it towards the lift.

The lift was an old thing, clanking and groaning as it carried me up and down, its iron gates closing with a shudder. Each journey felt like descending into the bowels of the store, emerging into the bright, bustling world below only to retreat once more to the quiet, shadowed spaces above.

At first, I was quiet, unsure of myself in the bustling chaos of Marks and Spencer. The hum of customers, the sharp clatter of stock being unloaded, the constant flow of people—it all made me feel small, like a speck lost in a vast landscape. But it didn't take long before I realised there was no need to hang back, no reason to be the shy kid standing on the sidelines. It took a few months, but I found my feet, as you do when you're thrown into the thick of things. You either sink or you swim. And I wasn't one to sink.

The other young men working there were a good lot. Ron Seaward, solid and reliable, was in charge of the cake and bread section, always ready with a joke as he sliced a loaf or weighed out buns. Len Davies and Ron Corbett handled the fruit and veg, their hands stained from lifting crates of apples, potatoes, and everything in between. Then there was Howard Evans, a bull of a man, presiding over the fresh meats like a king surveying his domain, the sharp smell of raw beef and lamb clinging to him like a second skin. We all had our place, and soon enough, I found mine among them.

After work, a few of us would head out to the Regency dance hall on Mardy Street, Grangetown. The place was always packed, the air electric with excitement, the thrum of music pulsing through the walls. But let me tell you, with the exception of Len Davies, not a single one of us knew how to dance. Len, of course, moved like he was born on the floor, gliding across the polished boards with a grace that made the rest of us look like blundering fools. But we didn't care. We had our own kind of fun, even if our feet were as clumsy as two left boots.

Before hitting the dance hall, we'd make our way to the Neville public house nearby. The Neville was dark, gritty, and smelled of sweat and stale beer. We'd order a pint each, and though the beer was awful—bitter, sour, the kind of taste that made you wince—we drank it down. We had to. It was all part of the ritual, the way men proved their mettle before stepping into the fray of the dance hall.

Once the beer was in our bellies, we'd march to the Regency, ready to take on the night. We'd ask the girls to dance, putting on our bravest faces, hoping they didn't notice how out of place we felt. And even though our moves were terrible, even though we stumbled and tripped, there was something about those nights. We laughed, we sweated, we tried our damnedest, and in the end, that's what made it all worth it. The music, the lights, the girls—it was a good time. And we enjoyed every minute of it, clumsy feet and all.

Through these years my sister Margaret remained a figure of authority to me, a woman of nearly twelve years my senior, and in the eyes of my childhood, she was already fully grown, distant in her adulthood. She spent her days at Fulton Dunlop's Brewery, a vast and arching structure that loomed opposite the old library on Working Street. Its stones were worn by time, much like the city itself, and inside it, Margaret busied herself in a world I did not yet understand. On the corner of St. John's Square, in a small wine shop under the same name, she worked behind the counter, her hands always occupied with bottles and glasses, her life unfolding beyond the narrow streets of my own.

Margaret married Jack Shorter, a quiet man, strong and steady, with whom she made a home in the rooms of Avondale Crescent in Grangetown in 1936, before the war darkened everything. I remember those days, walking down from Rodney Street to visit them, a younger self trailing behind the world she had already claimed as her own. Theirs was a modest life, but it seemed warm and safe, and I felt the glow of it each time I stepped into their rooms.

Years drifted by like smoke from a train, and after the war, they moved to a council house on the Gabalfa estate, a place where the air smelled of rain-soaked earth and the grey of the city pressed down upon the sky. Margaret remained there the years having settled around her as softly as dust. Two children graced their lives: John, born in the early days of 1942, and Margaret, not long after, in 1944. They were lovely children, full of the promise and light that had not yet been stolen by the world. And now, as I look back, I see Margaret as both distant and near, her life always ahead of mine, a road long-travelled, yet familiar in its winding path.

She used to write to me when I was abroad, fighting in the war for those long three and a half years. I remember how I would wait for her letters, those small fragments of home that meant more to me than she could ever have known. There, in the dust and chaos, where time seemed to stretch endlessly, her words tethered me to the world I had left behind. My mother's letters came regularly too, her handwriting so familiar, and every now and then, she would send parcels—200 Woodbines, no less. I knew they must have cost her dearly to send all the way across the seas, and each parcel, when it arrived, carried with it not just cigarettes, but love, the kind that endures even when separated by distance and war.

Jack, during those years, was in lodgings in London. He may well have been in the Forces too, for he was never home, always away. He had tried to join up with the rest of us, eager, I suppose, to be part of that vast, shared experience of duty. But fate had other plans for him. His hands, skilled as they were, were needed elsewhere, in the rubble-strewn streets of war-torn London, repairing the bones of a broken city. There, among the ruins, his importance lay in rebuilding what others had lost.

And Margaret—how must she have felt, alone like so many wives of men in the Forces? The quiet ache of loneliness must have been her constant companion. I imagine her waiting in the silence of their rooms, days filled with uncertainty, nights colder for Jack's absence. She had her own war to fight, one of waiting, of hoping, of carrying on with nothing more than letters to sustain her.

I recall that after the war, in the years of 1953 and '54, I found myself often calling at Margaret's house on Gabalfa Avenue. It became something of a habit, slipping in for a cup of tea whenever I happened to be working in the area—fixing gates, railings, balustrades, whatever the job required. Her door was always open to me then, and we would sit together in the quiet of her kitchen, steam rising from the teapot, the air heavy with that comfortable sense of familiarity. We would talk, sometimes about nothing in particular, sometimes about the past, and those years when life had been uncertain, but our ties had held firm. I came to cherish those moments, the ease of them, the way the hours slipped by unnoticed in the warmth of her company.

But soon, life, as it always does, began to shift. Margaret took up work part-time at Bateman's grocery store, a small but bustling place where the days were filled with the chatter of customers and the rustle of paper bags. After that, I'd be lucky to catch her at home. More often than not, I would knock on her door, only to find the house empty, the windows dark, her absence a quiet reminder that the world had moved on once again. Yet still, when I did manage to find her there, we would fall back into the same rhythm, our cups of tea, our conversations, as though nothing had changed at all.

In any event I stayed at Marks and Spencer for a while, longer than I might have thought, moving through the familiar motions day after day. The work was steady, a world away from the chaos I'd known before, but in its own way, it was a kind of waiting. I stayed there until January 1942, when the letter came calling me up for service. The war had finally reached out and claimed me at the age of 19 years old, as it had so many others. And so, I left the stockroom behind, along with the skip and the clattering lift, stepping once again into the unknown, knowing that whatever awaited me would be a long haul from the quiet, orderly world of Marks and Spencer.

CHAPTER 3

THE WINDS OF WAR

Unrest grips the world, and the first flames of conflict begin to smoulder.

During those days of the war, we were more than just shop workers at Marks and Spencer—we were fire watchers too, standing between the enemy and the destruction of our city. When the air raid sirens screamed out across Cardiff, which they did often, especially in the day, it was our duty to clear the shop of customers with all the urgency the situation demanded. The streets would fill with people rushing for cover, but we'd head in the opposite direction.

Once the store was empty, we'd make our way up to the roof, where the city lay stretched out below us, vulnerable beneath the grey sky. Up there, we'd watch the skies for the German bombers, their engines a distant rumble like thunder on the horizon. Our job was simple but vital—if an incendiary bomb dropped, we had to be ready to act fast, to snuff it out before it turned the building into an inferno.

But it was the night shifts that I liked best. There was something about the quiet, the stillness of the empty shop, that made those nights feel different. With no shoppers to worry about, we had the place to ourselves. The silence was punctuated only by the distant hum of the bombers as they crossed the Channel, their payloads destined for our streets. The darkness was thick, and the blackout ensured that no light leaked out from the city, but up on that roof, beneath the stars, we were wide awake, senses sharp.

Cardiff wasn't spared the wrath of the Luftwaffe. The bombers came both day and night, dropping their deadly cargo indiscriminately across the city. I remember the sky lit up with fire more than once, the horizon glowing orange as buildings burned, streets turned to rubble. It was hard to tell what would be left standing by morning. But up on that roof, there was a strange sense of purpose. We weren't soldiers on the front lines, but we were still fighting our own battle, protecting what we could, keeping a watchful eye on the sky for the flames that could turn the city to ash.

In those moments, under the night sky with only the distant rumble of bombers and the crackle of radio reports for company, it was easy to forget the world beyond the walls of the store. We were all that stood between the fire and the city, and that, somehow, made the night shifts the ones I looked forward to the most.

One evening, I was in the Central cinema with my mother when the big Screen caught fire at the back. Then we heard the air raid siren going. There was a panic everyone started to rush towards the exit, I stopped my mother and made her wait until the rush died down. She wanted to go so I had to go with her. When we got to the roadside a lot of buildings were on fire around us and it was as bright as daylight. We could hear the bombers and the Ack, Ack guns firing at them, and see search lights up in the sky. Shrapnel was falling all round us we could hear it the bouncing on the roofs and on the pavements. My poor mother was rushing home as fast as we could go without tripping over sand bags in the street. She was holding her black straw hat on her head thinking that it would stop the shrapnel from piercing the head. When we got home, we would go under the stairs in case the house collapsed. That was the safest and only place to go. Sheila, Bet and Alice had gone to Aunt Julie's cellar across the street but my mother wanted to stay in our house.

My brother Tom had always had the soldier's spirit, even before the war. He joined the Territorial Army young, eager to do his bit, long before anyone imagined the storm that was brewing. When the war finally broke out on that fateful day—September 3rd, 1939—Tom was already away in camp. We didn't know it at the time, but that was the last we'd see of him as a free man for a long time. There was no coming home after war was declared; he had to stay on, absorbed into the Army like so many others. He was assigned to the Signal Corps, where his job was to keep the lines of communication open amidst the chaos.

John, my eldest brother, had been living in London when the news broke. He was immediately called back into the Welsh Guards, and soon after, he found himself shipped off to France. He got caught up in the bloody whirlwind that was Dunkirk—one of the lucky ones to make it out in that desperate escape, fighting tooth and nail to survive.

Then there was Danny. He was packed off to Burma with the artillery, where the jungle was a different kind of enemy. Disease, heat, and relentless fighting made his war one of pure endurance. Burma was a hell all its own, but Danny was tough as nails and never complained, the letters began coming less frequently, the silence heavy with worry.

As for Alice's husband, Rob Stratford, he ended up in Libya, driving tanks through the never-ending desert, with the heat pounding down and sandstorms howling across the battlefield. Meanwhile, Bet married Len Price, who was shipped out to the Far East. His fate was perhaps the hardest of all—taken prisoner of war for three and a half years. Three and a half years of unspeakable hardship, trapped in the hellish conditions of those camps, surviving on scraps and sheer grit. Len was with the artillery corps, but no gun or shell could have prepared him for what he went through.

Our sister Mary's husband, John, went into the Pioneer Corps, another piece in the great war machine, building and repairing what the bombs left behind. Then there was Cissy's husband, Jack, who fought in Crete and Libya also with the artillery corps. Crete was a brutal fight, the Germans raining down from the skies, and then in Libya, it was more desert warfare—hot, bitter, and endless.

Mags' husband, Jack, was the only one spared the frontlines, as a bricklayer he was tasked with rebuilding the bombed-out ruins, in London, left by the Blitz. He may not have been in the thick of the fighting, but the work he did was just as crucial, piecing the city back together, brick by brick.

Every one of them was swept up in the tide of war, sent to different corners of the earth to fight battles on land, sea, and sky. And through it all, we carried on at home, waiting for news, living with the fear that the next knock on the door might be the one we dreaded most.

In the fullness of time, war would take me to distant lands—Algiers, Tunisia, and finally, Italy—just as it had taken my brother John before me. We were both infantrymen, boots in the dirt, rifles slung over our shoulders, part of the great march of men sent to fight battles far from home. The war swept us all up, and my mother bore the brunt of it, her heart heavy with the constant fear that one of her sons might not come back. With four sons in the army and four sons-in-law also in the thick of it, I can only imagine the worry that gnawed at her day after day, for five long years. No mother should have to carry such a burden, but she did it with a quiet strength that still amazes me.

Of all of us, it was Betty who suffered the most. For three long, agonising years, she heard nothing from her husband, Len, who'd been taken prisoner by the Japanese. Those devils wouldn't let the prisoners send a single letter home, not a word to let their loved ones know if they were dead or alive. Betty was sick with worry, imagining the worst, day after day, year after year. Then, one morning, three years after he'd been captured, she saw his name in the paper. That was how she found out Len was still alive. The relief must have been overwhelming, but the fear never truly left her. They'd only just married, you see, just before he was sent abroad in 1941. Imagine that—barely a few months as husband and wife, then three years of silence, wondering if she'd ever see him again.

Tom, had been in the war since day one and was sent to Italy and North Africa towards the end of the war, in '44 or '45, when the fighting was grinding towards its bloody conclusion. He'd been away for years, a seasoned soldier by then, hardened by the long campaign.

As for me, I knew my time was coming. I had my medical examination when I turned 18, in 1941. They passed me as A1, fit as a fiddle, ready for service. I knew then it was only a matter of time before I'd be called into the forces. The waiting was almost worse than the going, that heavy expectation hovering over you, knowing you'd soon be sent off to fight in a war that seemed like it would never end.

We all had our roles to play, all of us caught in the grip of something far larger than ourselves. We marched, we fought, and we survived—or tried to. For those of us lucky enough to make it home, the war never really left us. It stayed with us, just beneath the surface, in every quiet moment, in every name we remembered of those who didn't make it back.

The war looked grim for Britain in those early days—darker than anyone dared admit at the time. The Germans and Japanese were winning battle after battle, steamrolling across continents with brutal efficiency. For a while, it seemed like nothing could stop them. When France fell, it felt like the end was just around the corner. The Germans were at our doorstep, and the bitter truth was that we had almost nothing to stop them if they decided to cross the Channel. Our army was battered, our defences thin, and Britain stood alone, vulnerable, like a lamb before the slaughter.

Had Hitler chosen that moment to invade, there's no doubt he could have taken Britain. The Germans had swept through Europe like a wildfire, capturing one country after another, while our forces were pushed back, retreating with every battle. The Luftwaffe was bombing our cities to rubble, and the nation was hanging by a thread. After France fell, the question on everyone's lips was: *When would they come for us?*

But Hitler, in his arrogance, turned his attention east, to Russia. He thought he could take the Soviet Union quickly, and once Russia was crushed, he would have the strength and resources to turn his full force on us. And make no mistake, if he'd succeeded, Britain would have been next. We'd have been overrun, and God knows what would've become of us. Slaves, most likely, under the Nazi boot.

But in a twist of fate, he underestimated the Russians. That brutal winter, the vastness of their land—it broke the German advance. And while they were bleeding out in the snows of Stalingrad, we had time to regroup, to harden our defences and build our strength.

Thank God the Germans didn't think we were worth the effort at that moment, because had they landed on our shores in 1940, there was little to stand in their way. Britain was battered, yes, but we weren't broken. We fought like hell, holding the line in the air over our cities, and by the time they did look our way again, we were ready. It was a narrow escape, and for a time, the future of our country hung in the balance. But Britain never gave in, and that stubborn refusal to surrender became the spark that turned the tide of the war.

I was awoken early one morning by my mother, her face pale, her hand clutching a brown envelope like it carried the weight of the world. She handed it to me, and as she did, she said, "Oh my God, they've put you in the foot sloggers."

The words hit me like a punch to the gut. At first, I didn't fully understand what she meant. Foot sloggers? I'd heard the term in passing, but it hadn't sunk in. It wasn't until I opened the letter and read the official order that the truth set in. I was to report to the Welsh Regiment—the bloody infantry.

The Welsh Regiment headquarters was in Maindy, a part of Cardiff that had become synonymous with the thud of boots on parade grounds and the bark of orders. And now at the age of 19, I was to join them. The letter made it clear: I was expected to report to Aylesham in Norfolk on January 14th, 1942. No ceremony, no preamble—just cold instructions. My future, laid out in ink on brown paper, was now in the hands of the Army. Along with the letter were rail tickets, as if to remind me that this was real. My time was up, it was time to follow my brothers, Dan was in Burma, Tom in the signal Corps in North Africa and later in Italy, John in the infantry in Italy.

At the time, I still didn't fully grasp what being in the infantry really meant. I hadn't marched for miles under a burning sun, rifle heavy in hand, boots rubbing raw against my feet. I hadn't yet slogged through mud-soaked fields, my legs aching with the weight of the kit. But my mother knew. She understood the unglamorous reality of the foot soldiers, the ones who bore the brunt of war. The ones who walked into hell and back again.

It didn't take long for me to learn what being a "foot slogger" truly meant. Once I arrived at Aylesham, the reality hit hard. We were infantry, the ones who would be out there on the front lines, facing the enemy with nothing but our rifles and our wits. No tanks, no planes to hide behind. Just boots in the dirt and the brutal slog of war ahead.

There's no glory in it, no heroic speeches or grand gestures. The infantry takes the punishment, day after day, slogging through the mud, the rain, and the blood, moving forward because there's no other choice. We were the ones who walked into the thick of it, and it was there, in the sweat and pain, that I truly learned what it meant to be a soldier.

But that morning, as I stared at the letter in my hands, all I knew was that my life was about to change. The war had come for me, and there was no turning back.

Six months earlier, I had walked into the RAF recruiting office on Frederic Street, brimming with that sense of naive eagerness that only youth and inexperience can provide. The air was thick with the smell of tobacco and paperwork, and the chap behind the desk gave me a look, the kind that said he'd seen a thousand men like me pass through those doors. I squared my shoulders and told him straight, "I'd like to be in the RAF."

He nodded, almost too quickly, and replied, "We've got plenty of vacancies for men like you." That sounded promising, and for a brief moment, I thought the sky might be my calling. "Good," I said, "what would I be doing?"

Without missing a beat, he leaned forward and said, "We're always looking for rear gunners."

The words hit me like a bucket of cold water. I didn't need to be a strategist to know what rear gunners were up against. They were strapped into the back of the bomber, watching the enemy fighters come screaming in, bullets tearing through the air, and nowhere to go. You sat there, facing death head-on with nothing but a machine gun and the hope that your plane could hold together long enough to get you back home. Most didn't.

Fortunately, I wasn't as reckless as I thought I was. I knew enough to realize how dangerous that position was. I looked the chap dead in the eye and turned him down, saying, "I'd rather stay on the ground, thanks."

It was a decision that saved my life, and I knew it all too well. After I had joined the Army I found myself stationed at the airfields in Norfolk, guarding the very bombers those rear gunners were strapped into. I saw firsthand what became of them—those poor souls. When the planes limped back from their raids, riddled with holes, engines coughing smoke, the rear gunner's turret was often a shattered ruin. And when there was nothing left of the gunner to bring back, they'd sweep what remained into a bag—pieces of men who had faced the sky, and the enemy, with nowhere to hide.

I'd watch them clear away the wreckage and thank whatever gods there were that I'd had the sense to stay on the ground. The sky might have been filled with adventure, but it was the rear gunners who paid the price. And I wasn't ready to pay that price. Not then, not ever.

I savoured that last Christmas at home, knowing full well that come January 14th, my life was about to change forever. There was something bittersweet in the air, the knowledge that these familiar comforts—home, family, the simple pleasures of civilian life—would soon be replaced by the cold reality of military service. But I didn't worry. All my mates, lads I had grown up with, worked alongside at Marks and Spencer, were being called up too. It was just the way things were. We were all part of that great tide of young men swept up by the war.

Most of them, the blokes from Marks and Spencer, were headed for the RAF. It was what they'd wanted—a chance to fly, to be part of that glamour and excitement. But not me. For some reason, they'd sent me to the army, straight into the infantry. At first, I couldn't quite figure why, but then it struck me. It must have been because I was built for it. I was more physically developed than the lads heading into the RAF, and in the army, especially the infantry, strength wasn't just a requirement—it was a lifeline.

Army life demanded more from a man, particularly when it came to sheer endurance. You needed a strong back and legs that could carry you across endless miles of mud and rubble. You had to be able to lift, to dig, to fight with a rifle or a bayonet, and that meant being in the best shape of your life. I thought I was ready. At just 10 stone 7 pounds, I had no fat on me, not an ounce of softness. I was lean, hard muscle from top to bottom.

I'd spent my life working on my feet, moving crates, stocking shelves, running between customers. That kind of work toughened you up, and it made a man out of you. By the time my call-up papers came, I knew I was ready for whatever the army had in store. At least, I told myself I was. The real tests would come soon enough, but standing there, enjoying my last Christmas, surrounded by my family, I couldn't imagine just how far those days of strength would have to carry me.

CHAPTER 4

THE LAST GOODBYE

**Leaving behind the familiar,
stepping into the unknown.**

I WOKE TO THE STILLNESS OF snow falling softly in the dark hours of early morning. It was a silence so pure; it felt like the world itself had paused. My nose tingled with the cold bite of the air that had crept into my room overnight, a sharp contrast to the warmth I felt cocooned beneath the thick bedclothes of my youth. I lay there for a moment, taking in the sensation, wrapped in layers of blankets that had held me through countless nights, through dreams both bright and dark.

This was home, a sanctuary that had shielded me from all the trials and dangers beyond its walls. The quiet sounds of the house stirred faintly in the distance, the comforting presence of my family close at hand. It was a world of warmth and safety, of love that wrapped itself around me like those very blankets, protecting me from whatever lay outside.

I could almost hear the soft breath of my siblings in the rooms next to mine, a harmony of life and closeness that was as familiar to me as my own skin. In that moment, before the demands of the day took hold, I felt untouchable, as if the harshness of the world couldn't reach me here. Here, in this place of childhood memories, I was safe—safe from war, from fear, from the unknown futures that awaited each of us. But deep down, I knew that this was the last winter I would wake in this way, surrounded by all that had made me who I was. The snow fell softly, oblivious to the fact that soon, I would be gone, far from this warmth, into a world as cold as the air that now kissed my skin.

It was good to feel this way, swathed in the warmth of my past, though I could not yet grasp how fleeting it all was. In time, I would come to understand just how much I had—and how much I would lose. Life has a way of taking you unawares, throwing you into its savage currents, raw and unprepared for the bitterness that awaits. But even as it tears you from all that you know, it leaves behind echoes of what shaped you. Those memories—of love, of family, of childhood—would become my anchor, the strength I'd draw upon when the world turned dark and unforgiving.

I didn't know it then, but the turmoil that lay ahead would test me, burn away the softness of youth, leaving behind something harder, something forged by the fires of experience. Yet through it all, the sweetness of those early years would remain, a whisper in my soul, reminding me of who I was, of the strength that had been nurtured in me from the beginning. It was that strength, that unyielding core, that would see me through the battles—both within and without—carrying me across the jagged landscape of life's trials. And though much would be lost, I would emerge tempered, ready for whatever storms awaited.

As I lay there, in the warmth of my bed, I dared myself to throw off the covers and face the biting cold of my room. Outside, the world was still, but within the house, I could hear the familiar clatter of the kettle and saucepan as my mother prepared porridge, her quiet way of holding on to the morning routine, even though this day was unlike any other. Today, for the first time in my life, I was leaving home. The thought gnawed at me, filling me with a strange mixture of excitement and dread.

It was 4:30 a.m., the darkness still thick outside, and I lay there, staring at the ceiling, my mind racing ahead into the unknown. My heart pounded, not from the cold, but from something deeper, something primal—like the moments before plunging headfirst into uncharted waters. I felt the same sharp edge of fear, the same trepidation that comes before your first unaided leap. I knew the moment I left the warmth of my childhood bed; nothing would ever be the same again.

Today, I would go to war.

The thought hung in the air, heavy as lead. I tried to calm myself, thinking of my sisters, still fast asleep in their rooms. My mother moved quietly in the kitchen, her footsteps soft yet steady, as if preparing for the inevitable with the same quiet grace she'd always shown. I could smell the porridge she was making, the scent familiar, comforting. Yet I knew that after today, even those small comforts would be left behind.

I was no longer a boy, safe within the walls of my family's embrace. The world was waiting outside, raw and merciless, and today was the day I would step into it.

It was the 14th of January, 1942, and the bitter chill just before dawn bit through my coat as I stood on the doorstep of our home at number 7 Rodney Street, Cardiff. The world was still wrapped in darkness, but the snow had fallen during the night, settling in a pristine layer on the pavement. It lay undisturbed, the only witness to the quiet farewell that played out in the cold.

I turned to face my mother. Her eyes were red-rimmed, her face drawn with heartbreak that she tried valiantly to hide. She had seen this day coming, we all had, but nothing could have prepared her for it. I kissed her on the cheek, and in that moment, the weight of her sorrow pressed against me, heavy as the snow underfoot. Her arms lingered around me for just a moment longer, as if she could somehow keep me there, a boy, safe under her roof. But she let go, as mothers must.

Standing there, on that doorstep, I knew I was leaving not just a house, but the life I had known, the warmth of home, the comfort of family. Beyond the walls of number 7, war awaited. My mother whispered a goodbye, her breath a cloud in the cold morning air, and I gave her one last look before stepping into the snow, feeling the crunch beneath my boots.

Waiting for me just a stone's throw away was Mike Geen, a mate from Adam Street. His face was set, grim as mine, though it wasn't just his home he was leaving behind. Beside him stood his wife, her face pale in the half-light of the street lamp. She clung to his arm, her eyes brimming with unshed tears, but she stood silent, resolute. There was nothing left to say.

The snow around us softened the world, muffling the sounds of the city still asleep. As I walked toward Mike, I glanced back at the house one last time. My mother was still standing there, her form a shadow against the pale glow of the streetlamp, and I wondered if I would ever see her again.

I joined Mike, nodded a silent greeting, and we turned our backs on Cardiff. We were men now, marching into the unknown, bound for war.

We were heading to the same unit, Mike and I, both assigned to the 18th Battalion of the Welsh Regiment, stationed somewhere in the distant reaches of Norfolk. In all my nineteen years, I had never ventured beyond the streets of Cardiff. The idea of leaving home, leaving behind everything I knew, was beyond my understanding at the time. It was a distance that felt almost abstract, a stretch of land on a map, rather than the emotional chasm it would later become.

Yet in the arrogance of youth, that didn't trouble me. The call of adventure, the pull of something greater, eclipsed any fear or sense of loss. The reality of what it meant to be far from home, far from the comforting embrace of family and the familiar streets of home, was lost on me. All I saw then was the chance to leap into the unknown, to prove myself, to embrace the world beyond Cardiff as though it were mine for the taking.

It was a recklessness born from youth, a blind compulsion to explore every opportunity, to wring the last drop of experience from life, no matter the cost. I left behind my family, the warmth of my mother's kitchen, the laughter of my brothers and sisters, without fully grasping the gravity of it all. The true value of those simple, cherished moments—the ones I was trading away for a soldier's uniform—would only become clear with the passing of time and the brutal clarity that experience brings.

At that moment, as Mike and I trudged into the cold, we were not thinking of what we might lose. Only of what lay ahead. We were invincible, or so we thought. The pain of leaving, the ache of separation, were dull embers in our hearts, barely smouldering beneath the excitement and fear.

The world was opening before us, and we were eager to meet it head-on, unaware that it would, in time, break us down and mould us into something entirely different.

We boarded the 6:15 a.m. train from Cardiff General Station, a throng of young men like myself, all pressed into service by the unabated march of war. The platform was alive with noise—laughter, shouts, and the hurried farewells of families who clung to us in those last few moments. I looked around at the faces of the men who stood alongside me, lads from every corner of Cardiff, some I knew, others I had only just met. The mood was boisterous, filled with forced bravado, but I could see the flickers of fear beneath their eyes, the same fear that gnawed at my gut.

As the train lurched forward with a shrill whistle, pulling us away from the city we'd known all our lives, the noise grew louder. It was as if we were all trying to drown out the truth of what was happening with the sound of our voices. Some men laughed louder than the others, the sound brittle and hollow, while others waved frantically until their families became no more than dots on the shrinking platform.

I knew, as surely as they did, that beneath the laughter and the chatter, the same dark thoughts whispered in our minds. Thoughts of what lay ahead, of the dangers we were marching toward, and the cold, unfamiliar places that waited for us. But not one of us dared admit it. We were young men, Welshmen, and we had been taught to show strength, to bear the weight of uncertainty without complaint. So, we kept our fears hidden, buried beneath the masks of confidence we wore for each other.

I sat in the worn seat by the window, the landscape of Cardiff slowly giving way to the snow-covered fields beyond, and I wondered how many of us were thinking the same thing. That we were leaving behind everything we knew, stepping into the unknown with nothing but our uniforms and our pride to shield us from the storm that was coming. But no one spoke of it. We just watched the world rush past, pretending we were fearless, as boys often do before they understand what true fear is.

As the train clattered on through the snow-covered hills, the energy that had filled our departure slowly drained away. The raucous laughter and bravado faded into a heavy, thoughtful silence. Each of us, I imagined, was lost in our own thoughts, grappling with the reality of what lay ahead. The weight of it pressed on me like the cold outside the train, seeping into my bones. My heart was heavy, the finality of leaving home settling in with each passing mile.

I reached into my pack and pulled out the sandwiches and biscuits My mother had made for me, her love wrapped carefully in brown paper, her way of saying goodbye. The familiar scent of home—fresh bread, butter, the sharp tang of cheddar—offered me a small comfort, a reminder of the world I was leaving behind. For a moment, it was as if I was still there, at our kitchen table, the warmth of my family around me. But the illusion faded as quickly as it came, and the train's endless rhythm brought me back to the cold, unfamiliar present.

Mike Geen sat across from me, staring out the window, his breath fogging the glass. He had nothing with him, no comfort from home to ease the long journey. His wife's sad goodbye on the platform was still fresh in my mind, her face as pale as the snow we were passing through. Without a word, I handed him half of what I had. It wasn't much, but in that moment, it felt like the only thing I could offer—a piece of home, of warmth, in the midst of the bleak unknown.

He nodded his thanks, a small gesture, but in the quiet of that train car, it meant more than words. We sat there in the silence, chewing slowly, sharing what little we had. The food didn't lift the weight from my chest, but it eased the moment, a small solace in the growing tide of uncertainty. The journey stretched on, each mile taking us farther from the lives we knew, but in that small act of sharing, I felt less alone. We were all on the same train, headed toward the same unknown, but at least, for now, we had each other.

The train jerked to a stop at precisely noon in London, the steam hissing as if the locomotive itself was relieved to have made the journey. We gathered our rucksacks, the noise of boots thudding on the worn wooden floors of the train carriage as we stepped off into a sea of chaos. London was unlike anything I had imagined. It teemed with life and confusion, people darting in every direction with an urgency that felt unnatural. They moved like trapped rats, each scurrying with a singular focus, eyes forward, as if oblivious to the rest of the world.

The air was thick with the smells of soot and sweat, and the sound—God, the sound—was a constant roar, a blend of voices, the grind of machinery, and the ever-present thunder of footsteps. We stood in the midst of it, disoriented, like farm boys thrust into the heart of some strange new kingdom. My head swam for a moment, but the sharp bark of an order snapped me back to attention.

A pair of military police, stern and unsmiling beneath their peaked caps, swiftly took control of our ragged group, directing us like sheep through the throngs and down into the bowels of the city—toward a tube station. We were marshalled onto another train, packed shoulder to shoulder, and a lingering smell of damp wool and nervous sweat. The noise of the city above was replaced by the rumble of the tracks below, and we plunged into darkness.

Soon we emerged on the other side of London and were herded onto yet another train—a special one, they called it, bound for Norfolk. There must have been a thousand men or more, crammed into the carriages like sardines, enough to fill an entire battalion. As we sat there, packed tightly together, the weight of what was happening began to settle. This wasn't just a journey; this was the beginning of something far larger than any of us could have imagined.

The train chugged its way across the English countryside, the snow-covered fields passing by in a blur. When we finally pulled into Norwich, the cold air hit us like a slap as we stepped off the train. Sergeants and Corporals from the Welsh Regiment were waiting for us, their faces grim beneath their caps. They quickly set to work, barking orders, organizing us into smaller groups and loading us into lorries, each bound for a different village where we would begin our training. The world I had known—my home, my family—felt a million miles away now, lost in the smoke and steam of distant Cardiff.

We climbed into the back of the lorries, the engines growling to life as we jolted forward. We were no longer civilians, no longer boys with dreams. We were soldiers now, and the long road ahead stretched into the unknown, the first taste of what lay in store.

Mike and I were dispatched to Aylesham, an historic market town on the River Bure in north Norfolk, 9 miles north of Norwich. After fifteen bone-numbing hours of travel, the excitement of departure had long since faded. All that was left was the cold, confusion, and a hunger that gnawed at our insides like a persistent rat. The night had fallen thick and black by the time we arrived—9:00 p.m., but it might as well have been midnight for how dark and miserable it felt.

We were herded, stiff-legged and exhausted, into a mess room that was as cold as the night outside. The place was dimly lit, the shadows filled every corner, and the smell of stale food greeted us like an unwelcome host. A hundred men, each with the same hollowed eyes and sagging shoulders, stood around the pitiful excuse for a meal that awaited us. Barely cooked, the meat was grey and the potatoes looked like they had given up on life long before being served to us.

But hunger is a powerful thing. It drives a man to eat what he would otherwise scorn. We wolfed down the pitiful offerings, each of us silently hoping that tomorrow's breakfast would prove more generous, more substantial than the sorry fare laid before us now. The cold seemed to settle into our bones as we finished, our bodies too weary and minds too numb to even complain.

Once we'd finished our meagre rations, a Sergeant with a voice like a whip cracked orders, and thirty of us were marched through the freezing village streets. Our breath hung in the air, wisps of smoke drifting upwards as we trudged on, the frost crunching beneath our boots. We were led behind a shabby-looking pub called The Red Lion, where a barn waited, barely standing under the weight of years and neglect.

The billets were nothing more than a loft above the barn, accessible by a rickety ladder that groaned under our weight.

We were each issued a canvas sack, roughly six feet by three feet, coarse to the touch and smelling faintly of dust and old cloth. The Corporal instructed us to head down into the barn below and fill them with straw—our new beds. At first, the absurdity of it hit me. Straw, of all things, as though we were cattle being stabled for the night. But there was no humour in it, only the grim reality that we had entered a world where luxury was measured by the amount of straw you could stuff into a sack.

Instincts of survival, that primal urge to secure what little comfort I could, began to surface. I heaped straw into that sack with all the force I could muster, packing it down until it bulged like an overstuffed sausage. I had no illusions about where I was or what lay ahead, but I thought, at least, that I could sleep well if I made it full enough.

That first night, however, taught me a hard lesson. As I settled into my designated sleeping spot, already feeling the chill in the air gnawing at my bones, I realized my mistake. The sack, now round and taut with straw, became impossible to stay on. No sooner had I closed my eyes than I found myself rolling off the damn thing, over and over again, my body slipping off as if repelled by the very idea of comfort. I cursed under my breath and clambered back on, only to be thrown off again, like a man trying to ride a runaway horse.

The hours passed with me half-sleeping, half-tossing, until exhaustion won out and the straw began to slowly submit to my weight. It took days, perhaps weeks, for that sack to flatten enough to resemble something close to a bed. The straw mattresses reeked of damp and must, but none of us had the strength to care. As we lay down, the cold gnawing at us even through our blankets, I stared up at the rafters, the wooden beams looming dark and menacing above. The smells of the barn—hay, damp wood, and the lingering stench of old beer—mingled with the sounds of men breathing heavily in exhaustion.

It was a far cry from the warm beds of home. But this was war now, and the luxury of comfort had long since been left behind. Tomorrow, I knew, would only bring more hardships, but for now, sleep was the only escape from the bitter cold and the bleakness of what lay ahead.

But those first nights, they were brutal. In the darkness, you could hear the occasional cough, the rustle of straw, and, most heart-wrenching of all, the soft, muffled sobs of men who, like me, were struggling against the loneliness and cold. Some were just boys, still wet behind the ears, thrust into this unforgiving world with no more than a kiss from their mothers to guide them.

Their tears, barely audible but achingly present, spoke of homes left behind, of a childhood abruptly severed. In that darkness, we all felt lost, abandoned to the cruel machinery of war. But even then, none of us said a word. Pride kept us silent, even as the sound of quiet weeping filled the barn. It was our first lesson in the cold, harsh reality of military life—there was no room for comfort, no room for weakness, only the relentless grind of survival.

At 6 a.m., sharp as the cold winter air biting at our faces, we were paraded outside like cattle being herded for market. The sky was still black, the frost clinging to every surface, and the breath of a hundred men hung in the air like a cloud of smoke. We marched in silence, the crunch of our boots on the snow-covered ground the only sound breaking the morning stillness. Ahead of us lay the drill hall—what they laughingly referred to as the dinner hall—about half a mile away, our destination for breakfast.

Hunger gnawed at my belly, and every step felt heavier than the last, weighed down by the fatigue of a sleepless night. But there was no time for weakness. This was the Army now, and nothing would come easy. The meal itself was a lukewarm, barely palatable offering, but we wolfed it down without complaint. Survival instincts were already kicking in, and the need to fill our stomachs, no matter how poor the fare, outweighed any desire for taste or comfort.

The rest of the day unfolded in a flurry of activity. We were marched to the supply depot to collect our kit—our new identities in khaki. First came the uniform, stiff and smelling faintly of mothballs, its dull brown fabric poles apart from the bright, colourful world we had left behind. The Glengarry hat, perched awkwardly on our heads, marked us out as soldiers of the Welsh Regiment, though none of us felt like soldiers yet.

Next, we were issued two pairs of boots, each heavily studded with iron to withstand the miles of marching that lay ahead. The weight of them was surprising, as though they wanted to remind us that every step in the Army would be heavier than the last. We were also given black canvas shoes, the kind you'd wear on a quiet evening if such things existed anymore. Then came the socks—two pairs, thick and scratchy—along with vests, shirts, and underpants, all as functional and uncomfortable as you might expect from military issue.

The overcoat, woollen gloves, and grey denim blouse and trousers were handed out next—gear meant for the muck and grit of training. They would be our second skins in the months to come, dirt and sweat sinking into the fibres until they were as much a part of us as our own flesh.

We stood there in line, each man the same as the next, stripped of individuality, clothed in the drab, utilitarian garb of war. There was no turning back now. We had stepped into a world where uniformity reigned, where the clothes you wore were no longer a statement of who you were, but a mark of the machine you had become a part of.

I could see it in the faces of the men around me—the dawning realization that this was our new reality. No more warmth, no more comfort, just the endless grind of drills and orders, with these heavy boots and rough uniforms to remind us, with every step, that we were now soldiers, whether we liked it or not.

Then came the tedious ritual of re-confirming our personal details—a farcical exercise, given that we had already submitted them months before. Each man stood in line, one by one, now just another name in the register of war. The clerks, faces as impassive as the forms they shuffled, handed us our pay books. These small, unassuming tomes would soon become the record of our meagre earnings and the evidence of our toil.

The numbers were finally scrawled into the book—our weekly pay and the necessary inoculations that marked us as fully prepared for the rigors ahead. The pay, though paltry by any measure, was the only tangible reward for our sacrifices. We were to receive two shillings and sixpence a day, adding up to seventeen shillings and sixpence a week. In the currency of the time, this amounted to a mere eighty-seven pence in today's money—a sum that would scarcely buy a meal.

I had arranged to have ten shillings a week deducted from my pay and sent home to my mother. This was no mere act of charity; it was a lifeline for her. By designating her as my dependant, she would be eligible for a small pension in the event of my death. If I fell in battle, this pittance would offer her a measure of security, however slight. Without this arrangement, she would be left with nothing, bereft of any claim to support should I not return.

The irony was not lost on me—the sum that might one day sustain my mother if I were to fall was a fraction of what I would earn in a week. Yet, in the grand scheme of war, these details, these numbers, were small yet significant markers of the personal sacrifices each of us made. As we trudged away from the pay office, clutching our books and contemplating our pitiful wages, it was clear that the real currency of this endeavour was not the money but the resolve we carried into the unknown.

As twilight draped its shroud over the encampment, the call came for us to report to the drill hall once more. The chill in the air was a clear contrast to the steamy anxiety of the hall's interior, where we were to face the next rite of passage: inoculations in our left arms. The purpose of these injections was a blur, lost in the fog of apprehension and the ceaseless march of duty.

The scene that greeted us was a curious one. A sea of formidable men, each crafted by life's forge into robust, stalwart figures, now stood in line, their bravado swiftly crumbling under the weight of their fears. I watched in disbelief as countless men, their muscles taut with the strain of repressed dread, fainted at the mere sight of the needle puncturing the skin of the man before them. The needle seemed to take on a life of its own, a dark harbinger of the trials that lay ahead.

By this stage, we had all undergone the army's stringent grooming regimen. Our once free-flowing locks had been sheared into regulation cuts, a transformation that left us looking more like an assembly line of identical soldiers than the individuals we once were. The starkness of the buzz cuts served as a constant reminder of our new reality—a reality where individuality was subdued beneath the uniformity of army life.

In that moment, surrounded by a sea of fresh-faced recruits, our transformation was almost complete. The camaraderie born from shared fears and the collective experience of these rituals would bind us together in the trials yet to come.

Every dawn at 6 a.m., we were roused from our sleep by

the rigour of military discipline, and with a shiver of resolve, we marched half a mile to the mess hall for breakfast. This ritual was a rare moment of solace amid our ceaseless hunger, a hunger both born of our unceasing exertions and the voracious appetite of burgeoning manhood. The hearty meal was a balm, a necessary fuel to sustain us through the demands of the day.

Post-breakfast, we stripped down to gym shorts and vests—those scant remnants of personal comfort—yet we were mandated to keep our boots on for a six-mile jog. These boots, forged for the rigors of war, were stalwart and durable but weighed heavily upon us. With every mile we jogged, their weight seemed to grow, an oppressive reminder of the burden we carried.

The first week left us near collapse, our bodies on the brink of exhaustion. But then, like a beacon of hope, the arrival of plimsolls—light, agile, and infinitely more forgiving—lifted our spirits. These were our new allies in the battle against fatigue.

Our days were filled with rigorous training. We learned the art of drill, the precision of marching, the deadly efficiency of rifle fire, and the ferocity of the bayonet charge. Each lesson was a step closer to becoming the soldiers we were destined to be, forged in the melting pot of relentless discipline and the ceaseless march toward readiness.

Aylesham was a humble village, its character defined by a single main street that meandered through a smattering of narrow side turnings, a quaint and unassuming country haven. Yet, this tranquil village, with its modest charm, was forever transformed the moment the Army set foot upon its soil.

The surrounding landscape was a tableau of natural

fortitude, ideal for the rigors of Infantry training. Marshlands stretched out like nature's own obstacle course, while dense woods stood sentinel, providing both cover and challenge. It was this very terrain, rugged and untamed, that made Aylesham a strategic choice for the gruelling demands of military preparation. The village, once a peaceful retreat, now echoed with the unbroken rhythm of boots on its soil and the clamour of soldiers forging their destinies amid the raw embrace of nature.

For the span of three long months, we laboured under the malicious gaze of our instructors, honing our bodies and minds in the crucible of training. The days bled into one another, each marked by the gruelling demands of discipline and drill. At long last, a week's reprieve was granted—a brief respite that allowed us to return home, clad in the uniform of our newfound vocation, a symbol of our transition from civilians to soldiers.

Upon our return, the brevity of leave was but a fleeting mirage, as we were swiftly assigned to our respective Companies within the Battalion. These were Companies A, B, C, D, and the Headquarters Company—a hierarchy of military might each destined for its own role. We were dispersed to various airfields, each one entrusted to our vigilant protection. The looming threat of German paratroopers seizing these strategic points for their aircraft cast a long shadow over our duties. Our mission was clear: defend these vital positions with unwavering resolve, ensuring that no enemy force could lay claim to them and turn the tide of war in their favour.

CHAPTER 5

REVENGE OR FATE?

**A moment of violence—chance,
or destiny calling?**

I N THE STRUCTURED WORLD OF military organization,
each Company was a formidable entity, comprised of
four Platoons, each Platoon consisting of thirty men. The
hierarchy within was clear and rigid: the Platoons were
commanded by a Sergeant, adorned with three stripes of
authority, while each Section within the Platoon fell under
the watchful eye of a Corporal, marked by two stripes, and
a Lance Corporal, bearing a single stripe.

Every third day, one Platoon would be tasked with
standby duty, a duty that demanded vigilance from first
light until the edge of darkness. At the crack of dawn—
3:30 a.m. during the summer months—the thirty men and
their Sergeant would parade in formation, their faces set
with determination. They would then spread out across the

airfield's perimeter, eyes sharp and senses alert, ready to repel any German incursion.

The watch was unrelenting, extending from the early morning hours to the last vestiges of twilight, which lingered from midnight to 1 a.m. in the deepest stretches of night. This unyielding vigilance was crucial, for it was not just an exercise in discipline but a vital line of defence against any enemy that might seek to breach our fortifications.

The pre-dawn hours in those desolate lanes were a realm of biting cold and unrelenting loneliness. As the night stretched towards its darkest hour, the chill seemed to seep into your very bones, each breath a plume of frost in the dim light of your own fatigue. There you stood, half asleep and solitary, your rifle clutched tightly with a single bullet chambered—ready for the unimaginable.

At 4:30 a.m., the silence would shatter with the sharp blast of the sergeant's whistle. This was the signal to break from your vigil and sprint back to his location. The line of men would quickly form up again near the Nissan huts, our temporary sanctuary from the cold. The sergeant, a figure of stern authority in the dim light, would then direct us to perform a crucial drill. We were to work the rifle bolts, eject the bullets, and pull the triggers to ensure no live ammunition remained in our rifles.

Each man followed the command, the metallic clink of the bolts and the echoing clicks of empty triggers filling the air. Then, a single shot rang out—harsh and unexpected. The sharp sound pierced the frigid air, and the sergeant's gaze turned steely. He began his methodical inspection, bringing his nose close to each rifle, searching for the telltale scent of the discharged round.

When he reached mine, the air grew thick with tension. His eyes narrowed with fierce intensity, and with a voice that cut through the cold, he roared, "LEE, you're the culprit!" The accusation hung in the air, as sharp and sudden as the shot that had revealed my mistake.

Two men, their faces set like stone, marched me briskly to the guard room, the rhythmic pounding of our boots echoing through the corridor. The clatter of metal keys and the harsh scrape of the cell door being thrown open signalled my entry into the stark confines of the cell. It was a bleak chamber, furnished only with a hard wooden bed that promised no comfort.

Exhausted, I collapsed onto the bed and was quickly enveloped by sleep. The dark embrace of night was brief, and I drifted into a realm of fleeting dreams, where reality blurred into a hazy comfort. But the tranquillity was short-lived. The sharp call of the guards at 8:00 a.m. dragged me back to the waking world, the clarity of my punishment settling heavily upon me.

At 9:00 a.m., I was paraded before the commanding officer, who glared at me with a stern, cold gaze. The verdict was swift: seven days confined to barracks—a punishment that, in truth, changed little since we rarely ventured beyond its confines anyway.

In addition to my confinement, I was sentenced to a gruelling routine: every morning at 6:00 a.m., I was to appear on parade and toil in the garden situated in front of the office. This early morning labour was mirrored by the same toil at the day's end, an unstoppable cycle of penance under the watchful eyes of my superiors.

It was an unspoken truth that the young recruits,

fresh and unseasoned, were often preyed upon by the more experienced soldiers. Among them was a corporal in my section, a mixed race from Adam Street, Cardiff. His demeanour reeked of exploitation, and it didn't take long for me to catch on.

One day, I discovered that a brand-new pair of my army-issue grey socks had gone missing. My suspicions were soon confirmed when I saw this same corporal, seated with a needle and thread, darning the heel of a fresh pair of socks—my socks. I confronted him with my accusation, but he denied it with an air of insufferable arrogance. I lacked the proof to assert my claim, and his denial left me seething with resentment. The desire for revenge began to fester within me.

The opportunity for retribution arrived during one of our gruelling manoeuvres. We charged across a vast field, bayonets fixed firmly to the ends of our rifles. The mock battlefield stretched before us, a row of bushes with a stream lying beyond them. The corporal, ever the vainglorious leader, was at the forefront, shouting, "Follow me!" I trailed close behind, my 18-inch bayonet glinting in the morning sun.

As we neared the stream, the corporal leaped over it with practiced ease. I followed, but fate had a different plan. In my hasty jump, I tripped, and the point of my bayonet jabbed with alarming precision into the corporal's rear. The corporal collapsed onto the grass, his cries of pain a cacophony in the otherwise silent field.

A brigadier, an officer of considerable rank, witnessed the incident. His eyes fell upon the writhing corporal with a steely gaze, and he remarked dryly, "Perhaps you haven't been treating this soldier as he deserves."

From that day forward, the corporal's demeanour changed. The unspoken hierarchy of power had shifted, and I faced no further trouble from him or any others. The incident had not only settled a personal score but had restored a measure of balance in the chaotic world of military camaraderie.

CHAPTER 6

THE EDGE OF FEAR

**In the crucible of training, fear
is a constant companion.**

IN THE ROUGH AND TUMBLE world of the barracks, there were always those scheming to escape the grind of army life. Among them was a character from North Wales, a man with more cunning than sense. He claimed he couldn't speak English, though we knew better. On the parade ground, he would feign ignorance of our orders, pleading incomprehension to the Corporal's mounting frustration. When the Corporal's patience wore thin, he'd be sent off the parade ground, a temporary reprieve from the endless drills.

This man's antics didn't stop at linguistic deceit. He was notorious for wetting his bed, and his foul odour of urine became a permanent fixture. The medical officer, fed up with the stench, decreed that he should sleep in the guard room. To ensure he didn't flood the place with his nocturnal mishaps, the guard was instructed to wake him every two hours, urging him to urinate. Meanwhile, the ban on drinking after 8.00 p.m. was a mere suggestion to him. He would sneak out to the local pub for a few pints, a habit the guards turned a blind eye to, resulting in his bed and clothes being perpetually soaked and reeking every morning.

His antics and disregard for orders eventually earned him the ticket he so desperately sought. His crafty manoeuvring and subterfuge paid off, and he was finally granted his way out, leaving behind a trail of discontent and disdain among his fellow soldiers.

In the rough and punishing world of military life, there were always those who sought to escape the constant demands of the barracks through devious means. One cunning trickster would perforate his ear with a pointed matchstick, enduring the pain for the dubious privilege of a medical exemption. Another would swallow a small piece of soap before seeing the Medical Officer, ensuring his heart raced at twice its normal rate, creating a façade of ill health that was hard to ignore.

There was also a man who, under the guise of poor vision, would continually bump into obstacles, providing ample "proof" of his supposed disability. He'd be sent for an eye test, where he would lie and confuse the optician's every attempt to diagnose him, resulting in his dismissal from the examination. Ironically, this same man could be found reading the newspaper by the firelight, his eyesight seemingly miraculously restored.

Such individuals, unable to conform to the rigid demands of army life, would find themselves labelled as problematic. This particular man was eventually granted his ticket home because no Sergeant or Corporal could tolerate his incompetence. Even in the barrack room, where he was supposed to be sweeping up, he would deliberately leave bits of paper scattered on the floor, making a mockery of his assigned task to further prove his "disability."

The crux of these deceptions was that once you started working your ticket out, it became a prolonged test of endurance and nerves. The charade had to be maintained consistently, often for months on end, and the strain of keeping up such pretences was a burden in itself. The path to freedom, paved with deceit, was a long and arduous journey.

The training was unrelenting, a brutal vessel designed to forge men into soldiers. Each day we grappled with assault courses that tested our mettle and stamina, our bodies weighed down by full kit and rifles that seemed to grow heavier with each step. The route marches began as a gruelling fifteen miles, and soon they stretched to thirty miles, an unyielding march through the incessant landscape.

We marched at a steady pace of 120 paces per minute—roughly four to five miles an hour—making a thirty-mile trek consume the entire day. Every hour, we were granted a fleeting ten-minute respite, a scant relief from the dogged grind. Each time we halted to rest our feet, the agony of starting again was excruciating. Our feet, throbbing and blistered, were subjected to the Medical Officer's scrutiny. With a sterilized needle, he would burst the blisters, a painful but necessary procedure to keep us moving.

After six months of such non-stop training, the prospect of two weeks' leave was a precious balm. My mother, eager to see me and assess my condition, awaited my return with a mixture of anxiety and pride. The harshness of the training was etched into my frame, but the anticipation of her welcoming embrace provided a glimmer of comfort in the trial of military life.

Around August, we were thrust back into the rigors of manoeuvres. Twenty of us were huddled in the back of an army lorry, the metal box rattling and swaying as we were transported to the mock battlefield. I sat at the tail end of the 10-cwt lorry, the hard wooden benches on either side offering little comfort.

The driver, reckless in his haste, took a corner too fast on the narrow country road. The lorry skidded uncontrollably and crashed into a stone wall with a bone-jarring impact. The collision hurled us from our seats like rag dolls. I was flung onto the gravel road and lost consciousness.

When I awoke, I found myself in St. Andrews Hospital, Norwich, my body a tapestry of pain and damage. My left elbow was shattered on the radius, my face a canvas of scrapes, and my left knee throbbed with injury. Unconscious for nearly twenty hours, my arm was soon encased in plaster, a gift of the lorry's brutal embrace.

After a week in the sterile confines of the hospital, I was transferred to a convalescent home, a grand manor house commandeered by the army. The change was a welcome reprieve. The food was a feast compared to our usual fare, and the apple and pear orchards were a hidden sanctuary. For a month, I savoured the relative luxury and peace, careful not to burden my mother with the news of my mishap.

In hindsight, I might have exploited the situation to my advantage, claiming persistent pain in my elbow to secure a downgrade from A1 status and escape the infantry. But youth and stubborn resilience drove me forward, and I chose to endure, returning to the grind of soldiering with a spirit unbroken by the ordeal.

Mike Geen and I embarked on a new chapter of our training: learning to drive. Mike, unfortunately, faltered in this endeavour, but I persevered. Our lessons involved mastering the Bren gun carrier, a small, armoured tracked vehicle designed for rugged terrain and harsh conditions. The experience was as tumultuous as the vehicle itself. My early attempts left a trail of havoc—hedges lay trampled and mangled, bearing silent witness to my clumsy efforts behind the wheel.

Though I never pursued a career as a driver, the war's end granted me an unexpected boon—a driving license issued without the need for a formal test. Such was the peculiar generosity of wartime bureaucracy.

Yet, amidst these mechanical trials, fate had a cruel twist. My time in the marshes of Norfolk, enduring relentless training in the sodden terrain, caught up with me. I was admitted to Coltishall Aerodrome's hospital for three weeks, suffering from acute bronchitis. (Coltishall was a fighter base, and famous pilots such as Douglas Bader and John Cunningham were based there, it was located approximately 12 miles northeast of the city of Norwich and 12 miles from the coast). The damp and chill of those marshes, so merciless, had claimed their toll on my health. The respite in the hospital provided a welcome break, though the brutality of the elements and the unflagging demands of training left their mark.

As September drew to a close, misfortune visited once more. We were deep into another mock battle, the chaos of simulated warfare swirling around us, when disaster struck. Our lorry, lumbering towards the assembly point, was rammed from behind by a vehicle in the rear. The impact was jarring, a violent shudder that sent several of us tumbling to the ground.

I landed heavily on my back, pain erupting in waves that left me paralyzed. The darkness of the night enveloped me as I was whisked away to an RAF first aid post, where I endured a fitful night of discomfort. By morning, the severity of my condition became apparent, and I was transported to the hospital for a thorough examination and X-rays.

The diagnosis was grim: the muscles along the left side of my spine had been torn, leaving me with a debilitating stiffness that rendered movement almost impossible. The hospital's cold walls became my world for a week, after which I was transferred to a convalescent home. The weeks there were a welcome break, albeit one shadowed by the knowledge that my battalion had been relocated.

By December, our unit found itself billeted in abandoned hotels along the Cromer seafront, a coastal town on the north coast of Norfolk 23 mile north of Norwich. Cromer, with its rugged coastline and steadfast charm, stood resolute against the tempest of war that loomed over England. The village, cradled by the North Sea, bore witness to three ferocious bombing raids that shattered the tranquillity of its cobbled streets, along with a multitude of smaller incursions that rained down chaos—machine-gunning tearing through the air like the wrath of a vengeful god.

The church tower, a sentinel of faith, rose defiantly against the skyline, its steeple piercing the heavens, while the pier stretched out into the churning waters, a welcoming arm that drew the eye of friend and foe alike. This striking silhouette made Cromer an easy mark for the enemy's dark wings. In the early throes of the war, as the Axis forces roamed the skies, Cromer lay perilously close to their path, a waypoint for bombers enroute to the industrial heart of the Midlands.

As the bombers returned from their missions, the village became a convenient dumping ground for their lethal cargo, a grim testament to the merciless calculations of war. With each attack, the ground trembled beneath the weight of destruction, but Cromer, in its steadfastness, would not be broken. The spirit of its people, forged in the crucible of conflict, burned brighter than ever, a flickering flame of defiance against the encroaching darkness.

The cold sea breeze howled through those deserted streets, amplifying the sense of isolation and abandonment that hung over us. The silence was as chilling as the winter air, a clear reminder of the turbulent times we were enduring.

That is but a snapshot of the harrowing training that forged boys into men. Those days, etched into my sole, severed the last ties to my childhood, casting it into the mists of memory. The innocence of youth, once vivid and tangible, was now a distant echo, summoned only in the rare moments of desperation when the past whispers through the veil of experience.

CHAPTER 7

PROJECT TORCH 8TH NOVEMBER 1942

Algiers, Tunisia and the Front Line

The first taste of foreign lands, where dangers lurk unseen.

IT WAS WHISPERED AMONG THE ranks that we were destined for India, a clever ruse to mislead any German spies lurking in the shadows. Our hopes of the exotic East were reinforced when we were issued tropical uniforms, but soon we found ourselves packed onto a train bound for Southampton. There, waiting in the dock, was the troopship cruiser "RMS Franconia," once a grand Cunard Star Passenger Liner, now converted into a vessel for war. In her former life, she'd carried a mere two thousand passengers in relative luxury. Now, she groaned under the weight of five thousand soldiers crammed into every corner.

The first few hours on board were chaotic. Below deck, the air was stifling with the stink of sweat, fear, and the overflowing latrines that struggled to cope with the sheer numbers. Men were stacked like cargo, fighting for space to breathe. But I was one of the fortunate ones. The sea, with its treacherous swells, spared me from the sickness that gripped most of my comrades. Everywhere I looked, men clutched their stomachs, their faces ashen, retching into buckets or whatever they could find.

I, on the other hand, was ravenous. The food, freshly prepared in the ship's galley, was a rare luxury in the chaos. The bread, soft and warm, tasted like heaven to me, while the rest of the men could barely keep down water. For four or five days, I feasted—clearing the plates of those too sick to eat. My appetite knew no bounds, and with each meal, I grew stronger, fuelled by their untouched rations.

The voyage dragged on for what felt like a lifetime, the convoy's detour designed to deceive lurking U-boats stretched the journey far beyond its natural course. Six weeks passed before we finally sighted land, the rocky coastline of Algiers appearing on the horizon like a distant promise. The journey, meant to carry us to India, had instead delivered us into the heart of North Africa.

But the endless days at sea had already changed us. We had been soldiers before we boarded that ship, but as we stepped onto the docks of Algiers, we were survivors, hardened by the cramped misery of the Franconia. And deep down, we knew the worst was yet to come.

Algiers shimmered in the midday heat, a mirage of promise as we glided into the harbour. After weeks on the suffocating decks of the RMS Franconia, the city looked like salvation. The brilliant white buildings gleamed against the cloudless sky, but as we neared the wharf, the reality struck. The scent of the sea was replaced by the sharp, acrid stench of a hundred Arab boys swarming along the dockside, their voices rising in a cacophony, shouting for money, cigarettes, anything we could throw. They were barefoot, their hands outstretched, eyes wide with desperation, reminding us that here, life came cheap.

What we did not know at that time was that we were part of a secret mission called Project Torch. The shimmering haze of a North African dawn was thick with the promise of conflict and the scent of adventure. The sands of Algeria whispered secrets of the past, while the horizon was alive with the shadows of men preparing for the tempest of war that was soon to engulf them. It was here, amidst the rolling dunes and ancient ruins, that Project Torch was delivered on the 8th November 1942—a daring audacity that would etch its mark in the chronicles of World War II.

As the sun crested the rugged mountains, illuminating the path ahead, the Allied forces—an alliance of nations forged in the fire of desperation—readied themselves for an invasion that would change the course of history

In the hearts of the soldiers lay a fierce resolve, an unquenchable thirst for victory. Among them were men from Britain and the United States, their camaraderie a blend of cultures, united by a singular purpose: to strike at the very heart of Axis control in North Africa. They understood the stakes—this was not merely a military operation; it was a battle for the soul of freedom itself.

The landings at Casablanca, Algiers and Oran were a masterstroke of military strategy—a bold stroke of the brush on the canvas of war. A three-pronged attack on Casablanca (Western), Oran (Centre) and Algiers (Eastern), then a rapid move on Tunis to catch Axis forces in North Africa from the west in conjunction with the British advance from Egypt.

Project Torch stood as a testament to the indomitable spirit of those who dared to dream of a world free from tyranny. It was a chapter written not just in the blood of soldiers, but in the enduring legacy of hope and courage that would inspire generations to come.

In the annals of history, Project Torch would forever be remembered—not just as a military operation, but as a beacon of resilience in the face of overwhelming odds, a reminder that even in the darkest of times, the light of freedom can never be extinguished.

When we finally disembarked the RMS Franconia, the heat hit us like a hammer. We were ordered to march— seven endless miles away from Algiers under a burning sky, sweat streaming down our backs. Our destination was a mosquito-infested swamp masquerading as a camp. The air there was cloying, and alive with the buzz of insects. It felt like another layer of torment, a grim reward for surviving the sea voyage.

Our kit, issued with the promise of India, was taken from us the moment we arrived. We handed over our tropical clothes—useless now—and in return, we were given short trousers and shirts better suited to the blistering North African sun. The change in gear was practical, but it only deepened the sense of confusion. One minute, we were being prepared for India, the next, stranded in this forsaken land.

The officers wasted no time warning us about Algiers, but for some, those warnings were merely a challenge. "Perilous" was the word they used, though it scarcely captured the truth. It wasn't the bustling streets of the city that posed a threat, but the journey back—miles of empty road where the night swallowed all light, and danger lurked in every shadow. The Arabs had a reputation here, one that was whispered among the ranks with a mixture of fear and contempt. They were seen as scum, sly cowardly muggers and cut-throats who would slit your throat for a few shillings.

Of course, some men couldn't resist the temptation to see for themselves. Three men snuck out after dark, reckless with curiosity and thirsting for excitement. The next morning, we found their bodies—stripped of everything, left like discarded rags in the ditches. The sight was enough to silence even the bravest among us. The reality of war wasn't just on the battlefield. Here, it seeped into every corner of life, reminding us that death could come from any direction, even from those who seemed too weak or desperate to pose a threat.

There were eight of us crammed into a single tent, stretched out on nothing but our ground sheets atop the unyielding, stony earth. No beds, no pillows, just the raw African ground beneath us. It wasn't much, but after a day under the relentless sun, it was a relief just to collapse. Nights were no respite, though; the desert cold seeped through the thin fabric, making the ache of the day's march settle deeper into our bones.

That evening, needing something to take the edge off, my mates and I headed to the camp canteen. It was a large Nissan hut, thrown together in a hurry, but to us, it was an oasis. Inside, they sold what we assumed was wine—poured out of old, round tin containers, the type cigarette tins came in. It had a rough smell to it, but after weeks in the desert, we weren't about to complain. We gulped it down, grateful for the taste of something other than sweat and dust.

It wasn't until we'd downed a few rounds that we realized the truth. This wasn't wine—it was cognac, and strong enough to knock a bull on its back. But by then, it was far too late. The warmth spread through us like a wildfire, making our limbs heavy and our heads light. The world around us spun and swayed, but the laughter came easy.

Soon enough, the songs started. Sentimental, foolish tunes from home. We sang them in ragged voices, our words slurred, but filled with the emotion we'd been too proud to show in the daylight. By the end of the night, there were tears running down our faces, not from sadness, but from some deep, aching homesickness that the alcohol had unearthed.

There, in the midst of a foreign desert, surrounded by men who had become brothers, we let our guard down. For a few hours, at least, the war, the fear, and the uncertainty melted away, leaving only the songs of our youth and the laughter that followed. It was a brief respite, but one that we would hold on to in the days ahead, when the hard earth and harsh reality of our situation would settle back in.

The last clear memory I had was being thrown out of the canteen at the stop tap, legs wobbling like a newborn calf, and somehow ending up in conversation with a commando. He was wrapped in head bandages, looked as though he'd crawled out of the very pits of hell itself, and I, in my addled state, had the nerve to ask him what it was like at the front line in Tunisia. He just laughed, a deep, hollow sound, and I don't remember much of his answer.

The next thing I recall was staring up at the night sky, the stars flickering like distant fires, cold and indifferent. For a moment, I wondered why I was lying on my back in the bushes, as though I had simply lain down to admire the heavens. I tried to turn over, to get up and make sense of where I was, but a sickening realization hit me—I couldn't move. Not my arms, not my legs, not even my fingers. It was as if my mind was locked in a body that had stopped obeying. Panic rose in my throat like bile, but there was nothing I could do.

I lay there, helpless, thoughts racing, my body limp and useless. It was the most terrifying thing I'd ever experienced, worse than any battle, worse than any injury. There was no pain, no warning, just paralysis. I started to wonder if this was what dying felt like—slow and silent, with the stars as witnesses.

Then, out of nowhere, a lantern bobbed through the darkness. Voices followed, one muttering, "Here's another one." Rough hands grabbed me, dragged me through the dirt, pulling me from the bushes like some discarded sack. They didn't care if I was dead or alive; they just threw me into the tent and left me there to sort myself out.

I spent most of that night gripping the front pole of the tent, on my knees, heaving up everything I had in me. The world spun violently, and every breath was a battle to keep myself from collapsing again.

For days afterward, I couldn't shake the feeling. Even when I was stone-cold sober, just drinking water or tea, it felt as though I was still stumbling through that night. My body had betrayed me in a way I hadn't thought possible. From that point on, I swore never to touch a drop of anything I didn't know for certain. And to this day, no matter what's come my way, I've never been as drunk—or as utterly helpless—as I was that night beneath the stars in Algiers.

After about a week in that mosquito-infested swamp, we were marched down to a railway siding, where the cattle vans awaited. These were no ordinary troop transports; they were crude, ironclad boxes meant for animals, not men. Each van was supposed to hold sixteen soldiers comfortably, but in the chaos of war, comfort was a distant memory. Forty-five of us were crammed inside one, bodies pressed so tightly together that there was barely room to breathe, let alone lie down or stretch. It was like an oven during the day, the heat rising off our sweating bodies and searing the air inside. The nights were worse, though. The desert chill would seep through the metal walls, and we'd shiver like leaves in a storm.

We fought amongst ourselves—first to be near the door during the stifling heat of the day, where we could gasp a breath of relatively fresh air. Then at night, it was a mad scramble to retreat into the back, huddling together to escape the icy draft. Sleep was impossible. There was no room to lie down, no chance to stretch our legs. We stood, half-dead, in that suffocating prison for over a week. Time became meaningless, a blur of endless discomfort, hunger, and thirst.

After what felt like an eternity, we finally reached the outskirts of Tunisia, pulling into a place called Philippeville. (renamed Skikda in 1962) it lies on the coast of the Gulf of

Stora, part of the Mediterranean Sea. The landscape is hilly and forested, with high ridges on both the western and eastern sides of the city. It was a relief to step out of that hellish box, to feel solid ground beneath our feet again. But that relief was short-lived. We were marched up to a new camp perched on a hill outside the town.

None of us had any idea what was coming next. We thought we were here as a unit, the Eighteenth Battalion of the Welsh Regiment. But the grim reality hit us soon enough. They weren't planning to send us into battle as a single battalion. We were to be broken up, scattered like leaves in the wind. The army was bleeding men at the front line, torn apart by the ruthless efficiency of the German forces just a couple of days away. They needed fresh blood, and we were it.

Instead of fighting alongside the mates we had trained with, we would be sent as replacements, filling the gaps left by the dead and wounded in other units. We were to plug the holes, one by one, a patchwork of men stitched together by necessity. It was then that we truly realized the brutal, unrelenting cost of war. None of us were special. We were just bodies, tools to be used and discarded.

Many of my mates and I volunteered to join the Light Infantry. The opportunity had come up when we were attached to the 46th Canadian Division, under the banner of the American First Army. Despite the name, it felt more like a British operation, with more of our own countrymen than Americans in the ranks. It didn't matter much to us, though; we were soldiers, and the fight was the same no matter the flag.

The choice to join the Light Infantry wasn't exactly

voluntary in the traditional sense. The only units open to us were Light Infantry, whereas the Welsh Regiment had been part of the Heavy Infantry. I didn't mind. In fact, the idea of moving faster appealed to me, until I realized what it really meant.

In the Light Infantry, you march at 160 paces to the minute, which translates to a blistering pace of around seven miles an hour. In the Heavy Infantry, the standard was 120 paces, about four miles an hour. It might not sound like much of a difference on paper, but in practice, it was nearly double the marching speed, and the strain it put on your body was unbearable at times.

Marching at that speed in the scorching heat of North Africa was like being thrown into a furnace. Every muscle in your legs and back screamed in protest, the tendons pulling tight with each forced step. Sweat poured down your face, soaking through the rough wool of your uniform and sticking to your skin like a second layer of hell. Your boots, already heavy, felt like lead weights, sinking into the sand with every step. There was no mercy in it. The sun beat down like a hammer, and the horizon stretched out endlessly, taunting us with the miles yet to be covered.

It was like learning to march all over again, but this time, under a whip. The old pace of 120 seemed like a stroll in the park compared to the sustained rhythm of the Light Infantry. You could feel your body breaking down after a while, joints grinding, muscles tearing, but there was no stopping. You just had to keep moving, no matter how much it hurt, no matter how much your legs threatened to buckle.

The price for slowing down, for faltering, was too high. We had to endure.

Now, apart from the incessant flies and the constant sunburn, we had more serious things gnawing at the back of our minds. The thought of going into the front line unsettled even the bravest among us. There was no glamour in it, no talk of glory—just a gnawing dread that grew as we drew nearer to the fighting.

We joined our new infantry company just outside Tunisia, where the German army, though battered, still fought ferociously to hold onto the last bits of territory. The sound of artillery fire was ever-present, a reminder that death was lurking just beyond the horizon. Every step forward felt like it might be your last. The tension hung in the air like a heavy fog, wrapping itself around our thoughts.

For two weeks, we held the line, our nerves stretched tight as bowstrings. The days were a blur of blistering heat, the nights cold and filled with the eerie stillness that only war can bring. The occasional shout, the crack of rifles, and the distant rumble of tanks punctuated the silence. It was a strange kind of waiting—waiting for something to break, for the enemy to push, or for our orders to move.

Then, just as we were preparing ourselves for the worst, word came through the line. The Germans had given in. They surrendered. We had been on the front line for a fortnight, and that was more than enough — long enough, and bad enough. The days and nights had blurred into an endless nightmare of blood and shadows. Each moment we stood on that cursed ground, we faced death with every breath. The stink of war clung to us like a second skin, the deafening roar of artillery our constant companion. By the end of it, we were hollowed out, not just by the enemy's fire, but by the relentless weight of survival. Men were wounded, some maimed for life by shrapnel and bullets. It was a cruel reminder that war never spares anyone completely.

But when the news of the surrender broke, I felt an overwhelming sense of relief wash over me. A weight lifted from my shoulders that I hadn't even realized was there. For the first time in weeks, I allowed myself to exhale, truly exhale, without that knot of fear in my chest.

We hadn't been in the thick of it long, but that fortnight had been enough to mark us. And yet, I was happy. Happy to be alive, happy that fate had spared me this time. The battle for Tunisia was over, and we had survived it. But I knew deep down, as we all did, that the war wasn't finished with us yet.

CHAPTER 8

INTO THE ATLAS

**The towering mountains hold
secrets, both ancient and new.**

F OR THE NEXT MONTH OR two, my company was tasked
with guarding thousands of prisoners of war—Germans
and Italians alike—in various concentration camps scattered
across Tunisia. It was a strange interlude, the tension of
battle giving way to the monotony of overseeing the enemy
we had once feared. They were just men now, no longer
soldiers, stripped of their pride and command. We watched
over them with the same discipline we would have in the
field, but it felt different—almost surreal.

After that, we were back on the railway to Algeria for
more training, crammed once again into those cattle vans
like livestock. We were being transported all the way back
down the line, past the now-familiar desolate landscape, to
a place called Blida a town in northern Algeria. It lies on

the southern edge of the Mitidja plain at the base of the Tell Atlas Mountains and is about 30 miles southwest of Algiers. French in character, the town is surrounded by orchards. We were camped outside the town on the Mitidja plain. It was a flat, barren stretch of country that spread out endlessly except for the imposing silhouette of the Atlas Mountains rising in the distance to the left.

Blida became our new camp. A place designed for training—flat enough for drills, but close enough to the Atlas Mountains to mimic the terrain we would soon face in Italy. It was preparation for the battles to come, a rehearsal on ground that could almost pass for the rugged Italian countryside. Yet for all its practicality, it was a place of discomfort.

The camp itself wasn't bad, spacious enough with eight men packed into each tent. We slept on the ground, of course, but by now we were used to that. What we couldn't get used to were the flies. The flies were infinite. They swarmed in black clouds, unrelenting in their assault. The heat and sweat drew them like iron to a magnet, and no matter how much we tried to brush them away, they would land again and again.

Even the simple act of writing a letter home became a chore. You'd sit there, trying to gather your thoughts, but the flies would never leave you in peace. They hovered over your face, drawn to the moisture of your skin, crawling over your hands and arms until the frustration made you want to throw the paper aside and give up. But you didn't. You couldn't. Those letters were the only link we had to home, and despite the flies, the heat, and the mounting pressure of what lay ahead, we clung to them like lifelines.

Blida was just another stop in our journey, another

stretch of training before the real test in Italy. But it left its mark, not because of the drills or the exercises, but because of the vast emptiness, the flies, and the endless anticipation of what was to come.

We lived on a pint of water a day. Just one pint, brought to our camp by water wagons under the burning sun. That pint was meant to last from dawn until dusk, and we had to make it stretch. I remember how we'd shave and wash our bodies with nothing more than the water in our tin mugs. It became an art, learning how to scrape away the dust and grime with only a few mouthfuls of liquid. There was no luxury of bathing, no relief from the filth.

At breakfast, we were given a pint of tea, and the same at the end of the day. That was it. Beyond that, there was no more water to be had. If you wanted to drink from your ration, you had to purify it with tablets, and even then, it was still filthy. It was full of tiny worms and God knows what else. Dysentery lurked in every gulp, ready to knock you flat and take half the company with it. Men fell ill regularly; the pitiless sun and the contaminated water were the enemies we couldn't fight.

The toilet was a deep pit dug into the earth, with a long wooden pole stretched across it. Twelve feet of balance, with no room for error. You'd squat there in the heat, praying for a little dignity, but there was none to be found. Everything about that place tore away the layers of comfort and decency we once knew.

My mother had given me a small plastic crucifix before I left, a symbol of faith and home, something to cling to. I wore it on a cord around my neck, hanging alongside my two identity discs. It felt like a shield against the chaos. But the cross broke, a sharp piece stabbing into my chest, and over time, the wound became infected. The heat and the infectious air didn't help, and soon enough, my chest and back were covered in large boils, each one oozing blood and pus through my shirt and vest. It was agonizing.

The medical officer tried to treat it, but nothing worked. In that climate, nothing ever healed. My skin festered in the oppressive heat, the infection spreading, leaving scars I still carry to this day. Scars that serve as a reminder of that pitiless place, where water was a rare luxury, and the sun bore down like the judgement of an unforgiving god.

A new young officer arrived from England—a 2nd Lieutenant with the air of someone who thought he had the world by the tail. He strutted around the camp as if he were cut from tougher cloth than the rest of us, his shoulders back and his chin high, full of self-importance. You could see it in his eyes—he fancied himself a war hero in the making. But in time, he showed us what he truly was—a coward, through and through.

The first sign of his foolishness came soon after he took command. He decided that our company, all one hundred of us, would march up the Atlas Mountains for training, as if climbing those towering heights in the blistering heat was a brilliant idea. He chose the worst possible time for it— high noon in the North African sun, with the day already baking by the time we set off at 9:00 am. The man had no sense at all.

Now, we were light infantry, trained to move quickly at 160 paces per minute, but the catch was, most of us had only ever trained as heavy infantry, marching at a much slower pace of 120 paces a minute. It might not sound like much of a difference, but it was. Marching at that faster speed, especially on a near-vertical climb, under the pitiless sun, tore through our leg muscles and drained us of energy like nothing we'd ever known. Even the fittest among us began to feel the strain within the first hour, our bodies unused to the frantic pace.

The higher we climbed, the thinner the air became, and the more our breath came in gasps. The ground was rocky and uneven, treacherous beneath our boots, and men stumbled often, fighting both the slope and the heat. Sweat poured off us, soaking our shirts, but there was no relief, no slowing down. The lieutenant barked orders to keep moving, to pick up the pace, as if he thought himself a general commanding a charge up some legendary hill.

By the time we reached the top, most of the men were beyond exhaustion, legs trembling, lungs burning. But not him. Oh no, he acted as if it had been a mere stroll, though I could see the sweat dripping from his brow, his face flushed with the strain he was trying to hide. He may have led us up the mountain, but it was clear as day that he wasn't the tough guy he pretended to be. He was hiding behind his rank, a boy playing soldier in a man's war.

The thing is, you can't hide cowardice for long in this kind of heat, with the smell of death always lurking just over the horizon. And it wasn't long before this lieutenant would show his true colours. That day on the mountain, though, he pushed us to the brink, and we learned something else— we learned that not all fools wear stripes. Some of them wear the shiny stars of officers, and they can be the most dangerous of all.

At the base of the mountain, we were sternly instructed

not to touch our water until given explicit permission. The reason, they said, was that there would be no water until we reached the camp at the summit. Yet, as the sun scorched the earth and our bodies laboured up the endless incline, every rest stop became a trial of willpower and desperation.

We were parched from the start, and the dry heat only intensified with each step. Our water reserves dwindled rapidly, leaving us with nothing but the dry ache in our throats and the crushing weight of our exhaustion. By the time we had clawed our way three-quarters up the mountain, our canteens were empty relics, mocking us with their silence.

In a futile attempt to stave off dehydration, we resorted to stuffing small pebbles into our mouths, hoping to coax out a trickle of saliva. It was a pitiful remedy, but it offered the barest semblance of relief. Our sweat poured down in relentless streams, soaking our uniforms, while the heat pounded on our heads like a perpetual hammer. With each step higher, the air grew thinner, the pressure on our lungs more pronounced. Breathing became a laborious effort, our hearts racing with the exertion.

Four agonizing hours passed as we crawled up the final stretch of the mountain, each step driven by the singular hope of reaching the summit. By the time we finally arrived, we were near madness with thirst. The lieutenant's orders felt like an insult to our suffering. We had endured too much, and our will to follow blindly had all but vanished. We ignored his commands, driven by the primal need for water that had become our sole focus. In our minds, he had led us into a trial of endurance that bordered on cruelty, and we were more than ready to quench our thirst, regardless of his orders.

In the shade of the mountain, we were a sorry band of men, our tongues swollen and parched, stubbornly refusing to move a muscle until we were granted the solace of water. Nearby lay a dry riverbed, a cruel reminder of our desperation. Armed with nothing but our army knives, a few of us dug frantically, hoping to unearth some elusive moisture, but the earth betrayed us, offering no relief.

In a moment of grim inspiration, someone remembered the tin of soup in our rations. With a mix of hope and desperation, we punctured the tops of the tins with our knives and drank the contents. It was a vain hope, as the soup was laden with salt, only adding to our torment and amplifying our thirst.

Our prayers were answered when a little Arab shepherd boy appeared, his herd of goats grazing idly beside him. When we asked him where we might find water, he pointed up the road. Driven by an unquenchable thirst, we surged forward, disregarding the officer's commands to march. We ran past him, our only focus the promise of relief.

As we rounded the bend, our hearts soared at the sight of a small, enchanting waterfall cascading into a crystal-clear pool. Our first instinct was to drink deeply, but we restrained ourselves, knowing that too much water at once would bring the dreaded colic, a cruel torment of the gut.

The water was pristine and untouched, yet our desperation outweighed our caution. The feeling of relief was profound, a welcome reprieve from the torment of thirst. For the moment, the waterfall was a beacon of salvation in our dogged struggle against the harsh elements.

Water Falls at Blida (Atlas Mountains)

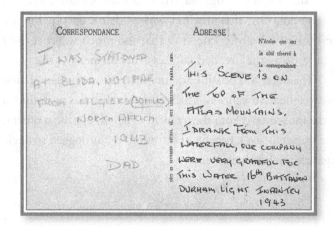

I WAS STATIONED AT BLIDA. NOT FAR FROM ALGIERS (30 MILES) NORTH AFRICA 1943

DAD

THIS SCENE IS ON THE TOP OF THE ATLAS MOUNTAINS, I DRANK FROM THIS WATERFALL, OUR COMPANY WERE VERY GRATEFUL FOR THIS WATER 16th BATTALION DURHAM LIGHT INFANTRY 1943

For three long days, we battled our way through the rugged mountains, pretending we were in Italy, taking on the Germans in an unmerciful terrain. The sound of real ammunition cracked through the air, so sharp and deadly that you didn't need to be told twice to keep your body low. Every time a bullet whistled past it was a reminder that this was no ordinary exercise. The weight of danger hung over us, even though this was only training.

At night, the mosquitoes were merciless. Swarms descended on us as soon as darkness fell, an incessant, buzzing army that never gave up. Sleep was hard to come by. You'd drop down wherever you could, exhausted and aching. One night, I settled myself on the side of the mountain, wedging into the uneven ground as best as I could.

When I woke the next morning, I was greeted by a sight that stopped my breath. Below me, nothing but a sea of white clouds stretched out endlessly. The sun, still low on the horizon, sent its first rays far into the distance, casting the clouds in hues of gold and orange. It was like gazing into heaven, so serene and otherworldly that, for a moment, all thoughts of war vanished. Everything was still, and the silence was unlike anything I had ever heard.

It felt like time had paused. But as the sun climbed higher, the clouds slowly dispersed, evaporating as though they'd never existed. Within an hour or two, the endless landscape below us revealed itself, harsh and untamed, stretching out as far as the eye could see. The world, once shrouded in mist, was laid bare again, and the battle that wasn't a battle continued. But for that brief moment, in those early hours, there was only peace.

The descent was a striking contrast to the gruelling

climb. It felt more like a leisurely stroll, the kind of walk you'd take on a warm afternoon, with the sun dappling through the trees. We followed a different route down, winding past a vast forest that seemed to stretch on forever. Our guide, a local, told us that the monkeys in this forest had no tails, and that this was the only place in the world where they lived. Whether it was true or not, I couldn't say. But the place had a certain mystique about it, a wildness that made you believe almost anything could be possible.

When we reached the foot of the mountain, we found ourselves walking through a sprawling French-owned vineyard. The smell of ripening grapes filled the air, heavy and sweet in the heat. As we trudged through the vines, an officer warned us not to touch the grapes, which was laughable. It was the kind of order that begged to be ignored, and naturally, we did. As we marched, we grabbed what we could reach, popping the juicy fruit into our mouths, savouring the brief burst of sweetness amidst the dust and fatigue of the day.

Of course, the officer saw a few of us indulging. He wasn't one of us. He was young, full of himself, and had no sense of camaraderie. Instead of letting it slide, he reported the men to the commanding officer, and they were fined for a petty act of defiance. The whole company hated him after that. His arrogance, his inability to understand the men he was supposed to lead—it was clear he was out of place.

We stayed on the Blida Plains for more training, days and nights filled with endless drills. We practiced landing on the beaches, under the cover of night, moving like shadows across the sand. Other times, we were the ones defending, trying to stop troops from landing. Every exercise was in preparation for the real thing—Italy. It loomed on the horizon like a dark, distant promise. We were being sharpened, honed for the battle to come. But even then, there was a sense that nothing could truly prepare us for what lay ahead.

CHAPTER 9

BLIDA AND THE ROAD TO BIZERTE

A deadly excursion through hostile terrain, where survival is the only rule.

E VENTUALLY, WE WERE ORDERED TO march back to the railway depot, and once again, we found ourselves jammed into those cursed cattle vans. It was the same routine, packed like livestock, with barely enough room to breathe, let alone move. The trains crawled along the tracks at a pace that would have made a tortoise blush with pride. The line was single-track, which meant that whenever another train approached from the opposite direction, one had to pull into a siding to let the other pass. The delays were endless. We joked bitterly that we could've marched faster than the train was taking us

In our platoon of thirty men, there were three lads from Liverpool—tight as brothers, and just as reckless. Together, they feared no man and no challenge, often pushing their luck in the most absurd ways. The train ride was agonizingly slow, the cattle vans cramped and stifling, and boredom gnawed at us all like a dog on a bone. But those three? They never knew how to sit still. Restlessness got the better of them, and they began eyeing the roof of the cattle vans like it was their playground.

John, the ringleader, was the toughest of the lot—stubborn and built like a bull. He was the type who always took things a step too far, and the others followed him without question. As the train crawled along, they decided to make a game of it, climbing out through the gaps in the doors and scrambling onto the roof. They played "follow the leader," hopping from one van to another as the train clattered over the tracks at a snail's pace.

John took the lead, bounding over gaps between the cars as if they were nothing but stepping stones. His mates cheered him on, laughing into the wind. But then it happened—he misjudged his step, slipped, and fell between the cars. One moment he was there, and the next, he was gone, swallowed by the grinding steel below. We heard a shriek, and for an instant, everything stopped.

His leg was caught under the wheels, and his body was dragged, bouncing across every sleeper, his cries of agony lost beneath the metallic groan of the train. His mates screamed for help, running along the roof until one of them reached the front, banging on the doors of the officers' compartment.

The train screeched to a halt, and we all piled out in a rush. The Medical Officer, a hard man with no time for sentiment, pushed through to where John lay on the tracks. His left leg was mangled beyond recognition, barely attached to his body. His face was a mask of pain, and he was begging, screaming not to cut it off. But it had to be done. The leg was gone, useless, nothing but a ruin of blood and bone.

The M.O. worked fast, his blade sharp and sure. With a single, brutal slice, he severed what was left of John's knee, throwing the wrecked leg into the nearest ditch like it was nothing more than trash. John's screams echoed across the tracks, haunting, unforgettable. We stood there, helpless, watching as the life bled out of him, knowing that from this day forward, nothing would ever be the same.

In that moment, the war felt closer than ever. Not just a distant enemy we were marching toward, but something raw and vicious, riding with us on that slow-moving train. For the first time, we weren't invincible. We were fragile, breakable—and that thought, more than anything, sent a cold shiver through us all.

When we were in camp, at least we could count on a hot meal every day, though it wasn't much to write home about. We never saw potatoes unless we wanted to pay for them. It was always the same—corned beef to fill our bellies, day in and day out. But when we were out of camp, like we were now, crammed into a cattle train for days on end, there was no cooked meal to look forward to. Just the same tin of corned beef and a packet of rock-hard biscuits that could crack a tooth if you weren't careful. Bread? We hadn't seen a loaf in over six months. The officers, though—they always had their fresh bread, something they didn't like to share.

Hunger gnawed at us constantly. I remember being so desperate I even tried eating unripe figs from a tree we passed by one day. Bitter, tough little things, but I was starving. I even chewed on grass at one point, hoping it might take the edge off, though it only left a sick feeling in my stomach. It's hard to believe, looking back on those days, the extremes we endured. The constant hunger, the discomfort—it's something you can't fully explain.

The train rumbled on, our destination this time was Bizerte, a small seaport village clinging to the rugged shores of Tunisia. The journey northward took us through a parched landscape, dust swirling in the dry wind, but we knew this was no tranquil outpost by the sea. Bizerte was a crucible of ambition and conflict, a launch pad for an operation that loomed larger than the horizon. An invasion force was gathering—thousands of men, tanks, and supplies, a tide of military might that stirred the air with electric anticipation.

Bizerte, the northernmost city in Africa, perched just 40 miles from the capital Tunis, lay at the mouth of a channel that linked the serene waters of Lake Bizerte to the tempestuous Mediterranean Sea. Its strategic significance was palpable. Once occupied by the Germans in 1942, it had been now been wrested back by the Allies, a pivotal moment in the theatre of war that granted control over the vital Straits of Sicily.

The Tunisian campaign—a brutal series of confrontations—had unfolded between November 1942 and May 1943, a desperate clash of wills between the Axis powers and the resilient Allied forces. British Imperial troops, bolstered by a Greek contingent, alongside American and French corps, had weathered the initial onslaught of German and Italian forces. But as the campaign wore on, the tide shifted, turning the vast desert into a graveyard for ambition. Supply lines choked, the Axis found themselves ensnared in a web of defeat, ultimately yielding over 260,000 of their soldiers as prisoners of war.

As we approached Bizerte, the air thickened with the weight of history, with the whispers of men who had fought and fallen on this unyielding soil. The stage was set for something monumental, and we were drawn inexorably into its heart.

When we reached our destination, we had to march six or seven miles with sweat pouring down our backs, the dust rising up beneath our boots and sticking to the grime on our skin. Thousands of British troops had gathered by the roadside, all lined up in neat rows leading into Tunis. The reason for all this fanfare? Churchill and Montgomery were to ride through in a victory parade, celebrating the British capture of Tunis. Though we were part of the First American Army, it was a British triumph they were cheering. We were there, standing at attention under the blazing sun for over an hour, tongues swelling from thirst. Every last drop of water in our canteens had been guzzled on the way.

Finally, we were dismissed. The order to break rank came like a blessing, and we made a beeline for a well we'd spotted in the yard of an Arab's house. The desperation for water had us half-crazed. We scrambled for it, like animals, but the Sergeant Major was on us before we could take a sip. He drove us away with a big stick, whacking it against our backsides and shouting for us to get back in line. A few corporals joined him, swatting at us like we were disobedient children. "You'll be sick as dogs if you drink from that well!" he barked. The locals might have been used to it, but our bodies weren't made for that kind of filth. Begrudgingly, we backed off.

Still parched, we started the long march to our temporary campsite, mouths as dry as the desert dust. The heat bore down on us, merciless as ever, until we caught the scent of the sea on the breeze. Suddenly, we could see the glint of the Mediterranean through a break in the trees. The shore stretched out, with isolated beaches as far as the eye could see. Someone in the ranks shouted, "How about a swim?" The sergeant looked back at us, saw the pleading in our eyes, and after a moment, he nodded. "Alright, lads. This way!"

We veered off the road, heading down a path hidden by a small forest until we reached a perfect stretch of beach. Without hesitation, we stripped off our filthy uniforms and plunged into the cool, clear water. It was heaven, that first rush of the sea against our sunburned skin. Naked and laughing like boys again, we floated and splashed, forgetting for a brief moment about the war and the heat and the hunger. For a while, the world felt simple, just the sea and the sun and the feeling of freedom.

Miles out to sea, a convoy of ships sat waiting to enter Tunis and unload their cargo. They loomed on the horizon, silent sentinels against the shimmering waters. The sight of them didn't interest us much then—Ernie Chamberlain and I were too busy enjoying the sea, far from the hard realities of camp life. We swam well out of our depth, at least a few hundred yards from the beach, the water cool and refreshing. It was liberating to feel the weight of the heat and dust slide off our skin with every stroke.

But then, just as we floated in peaceful silence, I spotted something. A dark, tapered shape, bobbing and weaving towards us in the water. My heart froze. "Sharks!" I yelled, the word tearing out of me like an explosion. I didn't wait for a second look. I turned and swam for my life, faster than I'd ever thought possible, arms and legs thrashing through the water like Tarzan himself. I had heard enough tales of sharks prowling these waters to know better than to stick around and investigate. Fear fuelled every stroke.

Ernie followed, but he was a good distance behind, splashing in a panic. My only thought was to reach the shore, feel the sea floor beneath my feet, and get the hell out of that water. When I finally touched sand beneath the waves, I risked a glance back, expecting to see fins cutting through the surface, hungry eyes tracking us.

But there was no shark. Instead, Ernie was shouting, his voice echoing over the water. "It's not a shark! It's just a broken boat front!"

Relief washed over me, but my heart was still hammering in my chest. We both swam back to shore, laughing nervously now, our earlier terror giving way to sheepish grins. We never ventured that far out again. The sea had scared the thirst right back into us, and as we stumbled back to the beach, the dry taste in our mouths returned with a vengeance. Swimming made us thirstier than ever, but that near brush with death—or what we thought was death—reminded us just how fragile we were in this brutal place.

We made our camp there, we slept in two-man tents, small and cramped, but enough to keep the worst of the elements off our backs. Before we laid our blankets down each evening, we made sure to check every inch of the ground for insects, especially one particular black beetle. This nasty little thing had the kind of bite that would make you curse every God you knew. What made it worse was that it had only one strong back leg, and it could jump three or four feet in the air—an unwelcome guest in a tent, to say the least.

In the dead of night, we were jolted awake by the eerie sensation of tiny legs crawling over our skin. It was pitch dark, but that didn't stop us from jumping up like madmen, tearing the tent down in a panic. We weren't the only ones. Around the camp, you could hear blokes shouting and swearing, tents collapsing everywhere as they fought off the night's invasion of creeping horrors.

The Arabs were always lingering around the edges of our camp, looking for whatever they could scrounge. Cigarettes, tea, sugar—they'd trade for anything. Some of the lads got clever about it, selling the Arabs packets of tea that had already been used, dried out, and stuffed back into the packet with just a thin layer of fresh tea on top. The Arabs, wanting to check the quality, would see the new tea and hand over the money.

Of course, they'd come back the next day, furious when they realized they'd been swindled. But they never got their money back. We'd just laugh them off, and they'd mutter curses under their breath, more frustrated than ever. Cunning as they were, especially at night, the game between us was constant. But it was always the same—both sides trying to outwit the other in this land of endless sun, insects, and clever tricks.

Back in the Blida camp, we had six men to a tent, lying side by side on the bare earth with only a blanket underneath us and another over our bodies. It was simple, almost primitive, but it was all we had. The nights were quiet, save for the occasional rustling of the wind or the far-off call of some nocturnal creature. However, the real danger came not from the wild but from the Arab boys who prowled the edges of the camp, silent and cunning as desert foxes.

They had a trick, clever in its simplicity. In the dead of night, one of them would crawl under the front flap of the tent, keeping low and quiet. With a feather or a light touch, they would tickle the nearest man's ear, just enough to make him stir. The poor bloke, half-asleep, would instinctively roll to the side, thinking it was a fly or some insect. That was when the boy would strike. He'd fold the blanket in on itself and give the ear another tickle on the opposite side. When the man rolled back, still clueless, the boy would pull the blanket tighter and slide it out from under him without a sound.

Bit by bit, he'd take the whole blanket, and in his stealth, he'd steal more than just that. Boots, hats, anything he could quietly gather, he'd push out through the tent opening. By the time the man realized he was uncovered, shivering in the night air, the boy would be long gone, vanishing into the dark with his spoils. The next morning, there'd be curses flying through the camp, but those young thieves were already halfway to town, laughing at their night's work.

It was a game to them. We soon learned to sleep lighter and guard our few possessions more carefully, but it didn't make much difference. Those boys knew every trick in the book, and they could rob you blind while you dreamt, leaving you cold and cursing at the dawn.

Next morning we moved camp to the nearby Mountains to wait till an invasion force of thousands had assembled. While we waited, the training didn't stop. Every day was the same. We drilled on how to invade beaches, storming them like the hell we'd soon face. Up and down hills, through dense scrub and jagged terrain, we trained until our muscles ached and our nerves frayed. Each night, as the sun set behind the peaks, casting long shadows over the valley, we'd drop to the ground, exhausted, knowing that soon we wouldn't just be pretending. The time was drawing near, and we could feel it, like a storm gathering on the horizon.

The heat and the flies were unremitting, the mountain nights cold enough to chill your bones. But we kept at it, pushing ourselves harder, knowing that when the time came, we'd need every ounce of strength and discipline we could muster. It was a waiting game now, and the tension was thick in the air.

CHAPTER 10

OPERATION AVALANCHE 9TH SEPTEMBER 1943

The Front Line Awaits

The roar of battle beckons at Salerno's shores, death stalks every step.

THOUSANDS OF TROOPS WERE GATHERING in camps in the hills outside the port of Bizerte, our embarkation point. Amongst them was a tension of waiting, the kind that made your muscles tighten and your senses stay sharp. Bizerte wasn't far from Tunis, and at night the Germans would send their planes to harass us. They came like spectres in the dark, swooping in low to strafe us with machine-gun fire or drop their bombs with terrifying precision. We had plenty of anti-aircraft guns of our own, though, and we weren't just sitting ducks. The sky would erupt into a dazzling display of tracer bullets and flak.

Every fifth round was a tracer—bullets designed to burn through the night sky, lighting up the heavens so we could see where the shots were going. It was a dance of death, the brilliant red arcs cutting across the blackness, followed by the loud explosions of shells bursting in mid-air. A couple of the German planes were brought down, spiralling in flames before crashing into the hills or sea. But there were always more, like vultures circling, waiting for a weakness.

It was in one of those nights, as we waited, that four others and I were struck down by terrible stomach pains. It felt like someone had taken a fistful of knives and was twisting them in my gut. We were taken to an American field hospital a mile or so away, staggering and bent over from the pain. The diagnosis came quickly—dysentery, one of the many grim companions of war. We were bedridden for three or four days, weak and uncomfortable, cursing our bad luck while lying on makeshift cots.

By the time we were discharged, the camp was empty. Our company, along with the rest of the assembled troops, had gone. They'd invaded Italy—Salerno beach.

Salerno, southeast of Naples, was the scene of Operation Avalanche, the codename for the Allied landings near the port of Salerno, executed on 9 September 1943, part of the Allied invasion of Italy. The Italians withdrew from the war the day before the invasion, but the Allies landed in an area defended by German troops. Its primary objectives were to seize the port of Naples to ensure resupply, and to cut across to the east coast, trapping the Axis troops further south. The Salerno landings were carried out without previous naval or aerial bombardment in order to achieve surprise. Surprise was not achieved.

The Germans had established artillery and machine-gun posts and scattered tanks through the landing zones which made progress treacherous, there were heavy casualties.

The news that trickled down to us was bleak. The Germans had been waiting, entrenched and prepared, and it had been a massacre. As the boats hit the shores, machine guns and artillery tore into our men, ripping apart the ranks before they could even get a foothold. The landing had turned into a slaughterhouse

A lot of my company had been killed, brothers-in-arms whom I had marched and sweated with for months. The knowledge that I had been lying in a hospital bed while they were fighting and dying gnawed at me like a slow-burning fire. Survivors' guilt. But there was no time for mourning. Soon enough, we'd be sent into the jaws of war ourselves.

The five of us were shuttled to Salerno by the Americans in a small, battered gunboat, the kind that had seen too many fights and was showing its age. The boat cut through the waves, slicing the water with a rhythm that matched our unease. When we finally reached shore, we waded through the surf, each step a mix of relief and trepidation, dragging ourselves up onto the beach.

We were directed to a transit camp, a temporary chaos of tents and makeshift quarters. There, I had to report to the officer in charge, explain who we were, and where our company was supposed to be. There we would wait to find out the location of our company so that we could join them. It felt like a lifetime waiting for the word to come through.

Among the jumble of faces and voices, I spotted a very young lad from my platoon. He had curly hair and a look of bewildered relief as he wandered around. When I called him over, his reaction was immediate and raw. Tears welled up in his eyes, and he clung to me as if I were a lifeline.

The boy, no older than a mere child in the eyes of war, had deserted his post when the fighting grew too intense. He had simply dropped his rifle and fled, hiding from the chaos that had overwhelmed him. Now, faced with the stark reality of his actions, he was terrified. The prospect of being executed for desertion hung over him like a dark cloud.

He looked to me, his voice trembling as he asked what he should do. It was a heart-wrenching moment—a young man's innocence shattered by the brutal demands of war. I could only offer him a bleak reassurance, though I knew the truth was far harsher. In the unforgiving world of combat, there were few second chances.

The chaos of battle had overwhelmed the lad. The endless firing, the screams of dying men, the mortars and shells bursting like fiery harbingers of doom had shattered his composure. In a moment of sheer panic, he had lost all control, fleeing like a hunted animal. He had hidden in a hedge, cowering until the fighting had moved on. Only then did the grim realization hit him—his flight from the front line had sealed his fate, condemning him to a grim future of at least imprisonment for desertion, maybe worse.

I took him under my wing, offering him a sliver of hope in the brutal reality of war. "Stick with me," I advised. "When I get my orders to join my unit, you can come along and claim you fell and were knocked unconscious. It's the best chance we've got." We shared a two-man bivouac.

Our time in the transit camp stretched on. It was a few days and each one dragged by, each one a never-ending wait for word of our company. The first night, nature unleashed its fury with an electric storm of unparalleled ferocity. The sky roared with the wrath of the gods, and the wind howled like a banshee, lashing the camp with rain that seemed to come from all directions.

The mountain tops blazed with the brilliance of lightning, great balls of fire darting across the jagged peaks. The American ships in the bay were tossed like toys on the waves, their anchors straining as if to hold them against the storm's rage. A couple of vessels broke free, creating pandemonium among the anchored fleet.

The wind, a force of nature's wrath, ripped our tent from the ground. It soared into the sky, carried away like a discarded rag. We scrambled for cover, racing under the nearest vehicle, our hearts pounding with the adrenaline of survival. The storm raged around us, a fierce reminder of the raw power of nature that matched the ferocity of the war we were caught in.

Morning light broke through the remnants of the storm, and the sun's warm embrace quickly dried our clothes. Eventually I was told a small army core, just four men, would take me back to my unit, I replied that there was one more to take and they said OK let's go. Harry got in with me along with another two soldiers and we were soon climbing up a mountain pass.

The ascent was brutal, a jagged ridge that clawed at the very soul. For an hour, we struggled upwards, every yard a battle against the mountain itself. The air grew thin, biting at our lungs as the vehicle clung to the rocky outcrops, the steep incline relentless beneath its gnarly tyres. Then, without warning, the peace of the wild was shattered.

The deafening roar of mortar shells tore through the

air, their explosions sending plumes of earth and stone into the sky. The crack of machine-gun fire echoed through the jagged peaks, sharp and vicious, as though the mountain itself had awakened in fury. Bullets whistled past, the smell of gunpowder in the air. The world had turned into a battleground, and we were caught in its grip.

Our vehicle, once a symbol of our determination, now became a helpless beast. The tyres screamed in protest as the driver fought to maintain control, but the rocky terrain betrayed us. With a violent lurch, we were thrown off course. The wheels spun wildly, then with a sickening crash, we plunged into a deep ditch, the earth swallowing us whole.

The world spun into chaos. The sound of metal scraping against stone was drowned by the cries of men, the hiss of escaping gas, and the staccato rattle of gunfire. In the madness, there was no time to think, no time to react. It was every man for himself. When the dust settled, I found myself among the wreckage, the twisted remains of the vehicle scattered like broken bones. The others were gone—taken by the trap that had claimed us. Only Harry and I remained, bloodied, bruised, and alive by some cruel twist of fate.

We clung to the edge of survival, knowing that the battle was far from over.

Amidst the chaos, Harry had been struck in the upper right arm. His screams pierced through the din of battle a sound as agonizing as it was unceasing. I ordered him to silence, knowing that any more noise would bring unwanted attention. We crawled through filthy, swirling water for what felt like an eternity before finding refuge in the shadowy cover of a nearby forest.

There, I swiftly removed Harry's coat to assess the

damage. Blood flowed freely from the wound, and I turned to his emergency dressing—a small, crucial supply each soldier carried in the top pocket of his left trouser leg. I applied the field dressing with practiced efficiency, hoping it would staunch the bleeding.

With Harry's wound dressed, we faced the grim reality of our situation: Germans still prowled the area. We ventured through the woods to the next valley, seeking shelter in a small cave. Our respite was short-lived, as some local lads spotted us and fled, shouting "Englessi, Englessi" in alarm.

Our options were dwindling, we could go no further so we settled into the cave, waiting for the inevitable. After two hours of anxious silence, I heard a voice calling in English, laced with a distinct Welsh accent. I responded, and the voice identified itself as friendly, promising to enter the cave without cause for alarm.

A young man, no more than twenty-two, emerged from the shadows. He introduced himself as a Welshman from Porth in the Rhondda Valley in Wales. He had come to Italy before the war had erupted, visiting his father's family in a nearby village, and was unable to return to Britain as the conflict had escalated. He brought with him provisions— food and water for three days—and blankets to ward off the chill of the night.

In that dark, secluded cave, we found not just sustenance but a fleeting moment of solace in the midst of eternal turmoil.

We had no shortage of firewood, and with my army mess tins, we managed to enjoy hot soup now and again, a rare comfort in the midst of our harsh circumstances. On the third day, the Welshman returned with unsettling news:

a Fascist group was prowling the area, hunting for British soldiers. Under cover of darkness, he led us to another cave, one he claimed had a tunnel extending up to the top of the mountain.

He handed me a torch and advised that taking this tunnel would be our safest bet to reach the next valley. We thanked him and I promised to visit him in his hometown of Porth after the war, a pledge I hoped to keep. The distant approach of men with shotguns quickened our pace. "Let's move," I urged Harry. "If those Fascists catch us, we'll be handed over to the Germans."

We moved swiftly to the back of the cave and discovered the tunnel, a dark, daunting shaft that seemed to climb endlessly towards the summit. Without hesitation, we began our ascent. Twenty feet up, a ledge materialized, and upon it, an unexpected sight: a large black bear, soundly asleep.

I swiftly affixed my bayonet to the end of my rifle. Each soldier is issued a rifle with a unique serial number, a personal mark of ownership for the duration of service. Harry, however, had lost his rifle in his frantic escape, a loss that troubled me as much as his mounting fear.

I tried to steady Harry, but his terror was palpable and his shouting only served to rouse the bear. It growled, an ominous sound that reverberated through the tunnel, and began to lumber towards us. I fought to keep the beast at bay, stabbing at it with the bayonet and flashing the torchlight into its eyes to disorient it. The bear, confused and enraged, was momentarily deterred, allowing me to inch my way up the shaft.

Harry, driven by sheer panic, had already climbed

significantly higher. I followed, inching my way upwards, each step a battle against both fear and fatigue.

We climbed out at the top, cloaked in pitch-black darkness, unsure of our next move. As our eyes adjusted to the night, we spotted a small shed and crept inside. Only then did I dare flick on the torch, revealing two men sprawled on the floor. They leapt up in panic, but I quickly calmed them down, and relief washed over their faces when they saw we weren't German.

They lit a hurricane lamp, casting eerie shadows on the walls, and warned us that German patrols still prowled these hills. We were trapped behind enemy lines, they said, hiding among shepherds and freedom fighters. The Germans would show no mercy if they caught us. The men were shepherds themselves, living off the land and keeping low. They urged us to stay hidden in the hut for the day while they fetched food and news on how to reach the British lines.

The day dragged on, a slow crawl of anxiety, but by evening, a Partisan arrived with food. He spoke broken English, but well enough to explain that his group would lead us to safety come nightfall. At midnight, they returned for us—three Partisans, Harry, and me. The storm that greeted us was fierce—thunder crashing, lightning splitting the sky, and the wind howling like a mad beast. The Partisan leader smiled grimly. "Good," he said. "No German will risk this weather." But Harry and I had no waterproofs, only our soaked-through uniforms. That was the least of our worries.

We moved through the storm, scrambling over rough ground. We'd covered about two miles when a shout rang out: "Alt! Ve ist das?!" My heart pounded—German voices. None of us spoke their language, so we bolted up a nearby hill as gunfire erupted behind us. The Germans were close, and to make matters worse, another patrol was heading straight for us. Bullets whizzed through the rain tearing through everything around me. One of our Partisan comrades fell, shot dead. We returned fire, and one of the Germans dropped, his body collapsing in the downpour. That bought us just enough time. The Germans went to ground, and we ran for our lives, darting into the night.

The Partisans turned back to their village, leaving Harry and me to fend for ourselves. We ran hard, desperate to escape the danger, the sounds of gunfire and mortar blasts grew distant as we continued our escape. And then we saw them—British soldiers on patrol. They almost shot us on sight, but we managed to explain who we were. The Captain listened as we told him about the German patrol lurking behind us. He immediately sent out his men to deal with the threat and gave us food and a tent to shelter in until they could locate our unit.

By morning, Harry's wound had worsened—it was festering, the blood caked in his sleeve. They sent him to a field hospital, far behind the lines. He said nothing about desertion, just that he'd been hit and left wounded until he'd found me. His story held, and I vouched for him. There was no reason for anyone to question it.

Eventually, I rejoined my company. They'd been locked in street fighting around the suburbs of Naples. It was a grim scene—our machine gunner had been killed in the chaos. War had changed us all, but for Harry, the battles fought within him ran deeper than any bullet wound. Still, we survived, and as they say, all's well that ends well—at least for now.

CHAPTER 11

NAPLES AND THE PRICE OF BLOOD

**War leaves its mark—on the
body, and the soul.**

E VENTUALLY, I CAUGHT UP WITH my unit. They had
been fighting street by street, house to house, through
the shattered streets of Naples. The city was a graveyard, the
stench of death thick in the air. Every corner, every doorway,
could hide a sniper, a machine gun nest, or worse. It was
brutal, and the casualties had been heavy.

A Bren gunner, a tough lad, was picked off by a sniper.
The enemy always targets the machine gunners first,
knowing they could break a charge or pin them down. I
spoke with one of the two remaining lads from Liverpool,
his face hollowed by exhaustion. He looked at me with
eyes that had seen too much. "It's been a nightmare," he
muttered, his voice a whisper. His mate, one of their trio

was sitting nearby, staring into space, his body trembling with the shock of it all. Shell-shocked. The fight had ripped something out of him, something that no amount of rest would return.

Of the three Liverpudlians who had once stood shoulder to shoulder, invincible in their own minds, only one remained unbroken. And even he was cracked, holding on by a thread. War had torn apart their brotherhood, leaving them fractured in ways they couldn't even understand.

It's terrible what these senseless wars do to people. Young or old, it doesn't matter. It eats them alive from the inside, leaves them hollowed out, shadows of the men they once were. And for what? Some twisted notion of power, of territory, of revenge. We're all just pawns in the game, sent to do the bidding of men who never see the front lines.

A group of young recruits had joined us from Britain. Fresh-faced, barely out of their teens, it was their first time setting foot on foreign soil, the first time truly tasting the grit and grime of war. Their uniforms still looked new and their boots barely worn. They didn't know the ways of war yet, hadn't felt the cold edge of death breathing down their necks. Most of them didn't even know how to operate the Bren gun, one of the deadliest tools in our arsenal.

So, they sat in a rough circle on the dusty ground, while a corporal, hardened and scarred by too many battles, showed them the ropes. He explained it in simple terms: how to load the magazine, how to aim, how to fire. One of the lads, nervous but eager to prove himself, was singled out.

"Now you show me how to operate the gun," the corporal said, handing over the weapon.

The lad, trembling with a mixture of excitement

and fear, lay down in front of the Bren gun. His fingers fumbled a little, but he managed to slot the magazine in place, following the corporal's instructions. He grinned at his mate across from him, pretending to take aim. The poor boy, never expecting what would happen next, didn't even have time to flinch.

Without warning, the lad pressed the trigger. A stream of bullets tore through the air, ripping into his best friend who sat only a few feet away. It happened so fast, no one had a chance to react. One moment they were laughing, the next, the young soldier was lying there, lifeless, his blood soaking into the earth.

The sound of the gunfire still echoed when the silence fell. No one moved. All frozen, unable to process what had just happened. The poor lad who had fired the gun stared at the body of his best friend, disbelief and horror etched into his face. He let go of the gun and scrambled backward, screaming, his mind unravelling before our eyes.

They took him away soon after, to a hospital. We never saw him again, but I knew, deep down, that he would never be the same. That kind of mistake, that kind of loss—it breaks a man. It's the sort of thing you never recover from.

We were huddled together in a small farmyard, grabbing what little rest we could. The place had clearly seen better days—war had torn through it like a savage storm. The hayrack in the corner was teeming with rats, their scurrying a constant reminder of the filth and decay that now marked the land. Nearby stood the ruins of what had once been the village church, its stone walls crumbled by artillery, its sacred air now defiled by the ravages of war.

We lay on the cold ground, too exhausted to care much

about comfort. Our clothes, still heavy with the dirt and sweat of battle, stayed on us as we settled in, trying to find sleep where we could. Despite the rats, despite the ruin surrounding us, we dozed off, too tired to care.

Then, in the dead of night, a scream shattered the uneasy peace. We all jolted awake, hearts pounding in the sudden darkness. One of the lads, groggy and half-asleep, had pulled on his boots so he could go and relieve himself. The scream had come because, when he shoved his foot into his boot, he'd felt something warm and wriggling inside. It was a rat, trapped and panicked. He flung the boot away in terror, his shout waking the rest of us like a gunshot in the silence.

Panic rippled through us all as the squeaking of the rats grew louder around us. We couldn't see them—there were no lights, only the pitch-black night. But we could hear them, scurrying across the floor, climbing over the hay, their beady eyes watching us from the shadows. Every rustle sent a shiver down our spines. The dark seemed alive with the things.

We didn't rest well that night. Between the gnawing fear of those vermin and the cold bite of the war outside, sleep eluded us all. It was just another reminder that, even in moments of stillness, war found a way to strip away any comfort we could cling to.

CHAPTER 12

THE BATTLE OF THE VOLTURNO LINE (9-19 OCTOBER 1943)

Crossing the Volturno's Bitter Waters

Where blood mingles with the land.

R UMOURS HAD STARTED TO SWIRL, like smoke on the wind, that we were heading for the front line. We all knew it was coming, had felt it in the tense silence among the men, in the whispered conversations between the officers. Soon, it became official. We were to be transported to a village close to the River Volturno. The river rises in the Abruzzese Apennines and flows southeast entering the Tyrrhenian Sea at Castel Volturno, northwest of Naples. The river is 109 miles long and German forces in southern Italy used the Volturno as their line of defence after the fall of Naples, and sure enough across that dark ribbon of water, the Germans waited for us. The thought of it twisted in my gut, but it was no surprise. War had a way of always taking you to the edge, pushing you to stare into the abyss.

It was well known among the men, and I agreed, that a German soldier was as skilled as any British fighter. They were disciplined, tough, and well-prepared. No one doubted that when the moment came to cross the Volturno, it would be bloody. Our orders had come down—soon, we would face them on the other side.

The night we were sent to the river was a miserable one. The rain came down in sheets, cold and ceaseless, soaking through our uniforms and chilling us to the bone. It was pitch black, the kind of darkness that clings to everything and refuses to let go. A lorry dropped us off about half a mile from the river, and we were handed a ten-man boat to carry through the mud. My arms ached from the weight, but we marched on, determined to do what we had come to do.

My company had been assigned a critical mission. We were to cross the river, make our way about half a mile inland, and then strike. Our target was a small, flat bridge that spanned a narrow stretch of land. Capturing it would be vital, allowing our tanks to cross through the maze of earthen mounds that lay ahead. Without that bridge, the advance would stall, and the Germans would maintain their hold on this sector.

The rain continued to hammer us and after what felt like hours trudging through the wet grass and sodden earth, our legs burning with the strain of carrying the boat, we finally reached the banks of the Volturno. The sight before us made my heart sink—a churning, swollen torrent of water, the current fast and treacherous far more dangerous than we had expected. The river had burst its banks, and the current was ferocious, rushing by with a roar that drowned out our thoughts. There was no way we could risk launching the boat on that water. It would be suicide.

The officers huddled together, voices low and urgent, and then the call went out—a volunteer was needed. Someone had to swim across the river, a rope tied around his waist, and secure it to a tree on the far side. Only then could the rest of us attempt to cross, hand over hand, clinging to the rope for dear life. It was a job for the bravest, or perhaps the most reckless.

A young lad stepped forward, one of the new recruits, barely out of boyhood. His face was pale, but his eyes burned with determination. The rope was tied tight around his waist, and without a word, he waded into the water. We watched as he fought against the current, the river threatening to drag him under with every stroke. Time seemed to stretch as he struggled through the flood, but by some miracle, he made it to the far bank, half-dragged himself onto land, and tied the rope to a sturdy tree.

One by one, we followed. We all knew that once we set foot in those waters, there was no going back. We'd be on the other side soon enough, facing whatever hell the Germans had waiting for us.

The rain lashed against our faces, and we were already soaking wet, so the water didn't matter anymore. What did matter was the sheer will it took to keep moving, to keep hauling ourselves across that raging river, hand over hand along the rope. The current tugged at us, threatened to pull us under, but we kept going. Failure wasn't an option.

When I finally staggered to the other side, breathless and shaking, I turned to watch the last of my comrades make the crossing. We were all alive, battered and soaked to the skin, but we had made it. There was no time for relief, though. Ahead of us lay the real fight—the Germans were waiting, and we still had a mission to complete.

Time was slipping through our fingers, and we were still not in position. Dawn was creeping up behind us, and Mount Vesuvius loomed ominously in the distance, spewing fire into the night sky. It felt like the earth itself was angry, churning with the same restless energy that thrummed through us all. The rain had eased but left everything wet and treacherous. We were meant to be across and in place before first light, but the river had slowed us, and now we were dangerously exposed.

On the opposite bank, we finally gathered, breathless and soaked to the bone. As we waited for the command to advance, the sky above us suddenly exploded into brightness. German *Verry Lichts* streaked into the air, bursting like fireworks. In an instant, the darkness was obliterated, and the night was as bright as midday. The Germans had caught wind of our approach, and now we were as visible as sitting ducks.

Panic rippled through the ranks. "Run and follow me!" our commanding officer yelled, his voice cutting through the chaos. Without a second thought, we surged forward, tearing across the open ground like hunted animals. There were three or more fields between us and our target, and in each one, we were horribly exposed.

Ahead of us loomed a wooden gate, the only way through to the next field. But between us and that gate was a wall of open air—a killing ground. My heart pounded in my ears as we sprinted toward it, mud sucking at our boots. A machine gun suddenly burst into life from behind a thick hedge to our right. It wasn't aimed precisely, but that didn't matter. The German gunner didn't need to see us—he was strafing the fields with a cold, calculated sweep. Every fifth bullet was a tracer, glowing white-hot as it zipped past. You could see the line of fire tracing up and down like death's scythe, cutting through the dark.

We hit the dirt; bodies pressed flat against the wet ground. The machine gun fire raked up and down the field, keeping us tied to the ground. There was no point in staying put—the gunner would just keep firing, sweeping his bullets up and down the field like a blind man feeling his way with a stick, deadly and unrelenting. I could hear the sharp crack of bullets hitting the dirt, the occasional scream as someone was hit, but I forced myself to stay focused.

We lay there, divided—half of us to the left, half to the right of that deadly stream of bullets, pinned down by the German machine gun. The instinct to press ourselves as close to the earth as humanly possible gripped us all. The ground, cold and wet, was our only shield, our only protection from the torrent of death slicing the air above.

I dared to lift my head, just a fraction, enough to glance toward the line of tracer fire cutting across the field. The burning trail was just two feet from where I lay, so close I could feel the heat in the chill of the night. I could hear the sharp thud as those white-hot bullets struck the earth, tearing through the mud like an angry god scouring the land.

Suddenly, I heard it—*ping*. A tracer bullet ricocheted

off the heel of the one of the men, a sharp metallic crack that echoed in the madness of battle. In a blink, that same bullet veered straight into the throat of the poor lad lying just ahead of me. There was no time for warning, no chance for him to react. One moment he was there, and in the next, I heard his final, guttural sound—a low, awful "Aargh"—as the light left his eyes.

He was gone, just like that.

I pressed my head down harder into the muck, my heart pounding with the realization of how thin the line was between life and death. Just inches. A metal heel had saved one man and doomed another. There was nothing we could do but lie there, frozen, knowing that at any moment, any one of us could be next.

In war, death was always close. But here, in that terrifying stillness, with the sound of bullets slicing the air around us, it felt like death was breathing down our necks, watching, waiting for the slightest mistake. I held my breath and waited for the machine gun to stop, praying for a chance to move before it was too late.

How long we lay there, I couldn't say for sure. It felt like hours—time stretches in strange ways when death hovers over you—but thinking on it now, it was probably no more than fifteen minutes. Fifteen minutes of sheer terror, lying in the mud, listening to that unrelenting machine gun raking the ground, waiting for the moment when it would stop... or when it would find you.

What finally made us move was the growing certainty that the Germans would start lobbing mortar bombs in our direction. The thought chilled me more than the bullets. A rifle or machine gun you could dodge, you could keep low and pray, but mortar bombs were indiscriminate killers. They'd tear apart everything and everyone within their blast radius.

I glanced to my left and saw the telltale glow—those cursed six-inch mortar tubes, sitting back in the enemy lines, lighting up when they fired. It was like a flash of lightning on a stormy night, followed by a sound that chilled me to the bone. The noise they made... I've never heard anything like it. It was like the gut-wrenching retch of a giant, a deep, violent *vomiting* sound, rumbling through the night. And once you heard that, you knew you had only moments before the earth would erupt around you.

The first barrage of six mortar bombs exploded to our left, a deafening roar of destruction that tore the earth apart. The ground shook violently, dirt and shrapnel rained down on us like hail. Then came another volley, this time to the right. The message was clear—if we didn't move, the next salvo would land directly on top of us, and there wouldn't be anything left to bury.

Our commanding officer passed the word down the line. "Move to the gate. Wait for my signal," he ordered in a low, fierce whisper. We knew what that meant. The only time we'd have a chance was when the machine gunner on the other side of the field had to stop, to reload his cursed weapon with a fresh belt of cartridges. It was our only window, and it would be brief. Too long in the open, and we'd be mowed down like grass before a scythe.

I could hear my heartbeat pounding in my ears as we crouched, waiting. The relentless thud of the machine gun slowed, the moment of opportunity upon us. "Go!" the officer barked. In one desperate surge, we scrambled up from the mud and ran, heads down, weaving between the bursts of gunfire and mortar explosions. It was chaos. Men to my left, men to my right, running like rabbits fleeing a hawk. The air was thick with the smell of burning cordite and wet earth. Another mortar blast behind us, closer this time, sent chunks of earth flying, and a scream cut through the night. But we kept running. There was no time to stop, no time to look back.

We surged toward the gate, every man scrambling over it as fast as his hands and feet would take him. The second we cleared it, we found ourselves in a field of deep furrows, wet with rain and mud, a perfect place to hide, but also treacherous terrain. We threw ourselves into those furrows, crawling like worms through the muck, inching forward.

The tension was unbearable. Any sound, any movement out of sync with the quiet, could bring death raining down on us again. The mortar bombs had ceased for the moment, but they could come again at any time, tracking us as we moved. Each explosion behind us was a reminder that they were still hunting, still seeking out targets.

We crawled across four, maybe five fields—God only knows how far we went, my sense of time completely lost in the haze of fear and exhaustion. Every field felt like entering the lion's den. We had no idea if Germans were lying in wait, silent and unseen, ready to cut us down as we stumbled through the darkness. The uncertainty gnawed at the back of my mind. It felt like stepping into a cave, not knowing whether the beast was sleeping inside, waiting to pounce.

We kept low, barely breathing, each man praying to avoid the roar of mortar fire or the crack of a rifle from the shadows. Our lives hung by a thread, and that thread was fraying fast.

CHAPTER 13

FIRST DANCE WITH DEATH – THE BRIDGE

**Front Line and Foxholes, a
near fatal encounter.**

THE RAIN WAS INCESSANT, POURING down in sheets, and the ceaseless explosions of mortar fire had left my ears ringing, a cruel prelude to the hearing damage that would haunt me for years to come. Our squad, soaked to the bone and shivering, finally reached our position by a small bridge more like a flat bit of road with a tunnel underneath. The terrain was a grim battlefield of mud and chaos, and there, beside the bridge, our small section of ten men took up their positions.

The order came to dig in and prepare our defences. We had to burrow into the earth, carving out shallow pits to shelter our bodies and conceal ourselves from the enemy. The task was grim, but it was survival.

I chose to dig at the top of a high mound, a vantage point that seemed to offer a better view and perhaps a bit of protection. I reckoned that if the Germans decided to lob their hand grenades over our way, I'd be the first to swat them down the mound. With that in mind, I threw myself into digging a defensive hole with a comrade. We laboured side by side, carving out a pit about three feet deep, four feet long, and a foot and a half wide. It wasn't much, but it would have to do. Ernie, my mate, preferred the lower ground, arguing that it would offer better cover. We chose our places as best as we could, each of us driven by the instinct for survival.

The ground was stubborn and sodden, and our efforts were slow, the rain turning the earth into a thick, clinging mud. Every spade full seemed to weigh a ton, every movement a struggle against the incessant downpour. As we dug, the sounds of battle continued around us, a constant reminder of the peril that surrounded us. The bridge stood silent and ominous, the tunnel below a dark maw that seemed to hold countless dangers.

With the pits finally prepared, I clambered up to the top of the mound to survey our surroundings. The dawn was creeping in, casting a pale light across the battlefield. I hadn't realized how easily my figure could be silhouetted against the emerging light, making me an easy target for any German sniper lurking behind us.

Just as the thought crossed my mind, there was a sharp, jarring noise—Bang! My helmet flew off my head, and I plunged back into the pit, my heart racing. The bullet had struck my helmet with enough force to dent it deeply. I was shaken but otherwise unharmed. The danger was real, the sniper was out there, I spotted an Italian farmhouse and thought that must be his hiding place. It was not the last time that I would be his target!

In the protection of the fox hole, the whole world seemed to hold its breath as I huddled in safety, the weight of the battle pressing down upon me. We crouched into them, pulling the damp earth up around us for cover. The rain soaked through everything, but at least now we were hidden, our bodies shielded from view. We huddled there, waiting for the inevitable clash, our ears still ringing with the echoes of the mortar explosions

The corporal in charge of our section barked at me, "Lee, you and your mate head over to the opposite mound and dig in at the bottom. Take a Bren gun, hand grenades, and your rifle. If the Germans come, you'll be the first line of defence for our position."

I couldn't believe my ears. I looked in his direction, incredulous, and replied, "You can get stuffed I'm not that bloody daft". I was not about to put myself in such a foolhardy position."

He narrowed his eyes and said he'd report my insubordination once we were out of the line. I shot back, "Ay, if we get out of the line." The defiance in my voice must have struck a chord, because he begrudgingly sent two other men to take up the task instead.

As it turned out, they were promptly captured by the Germans. The fate of those two was a grim reminder of the harshness of our reality, and the irony of it all wasn't lost on me.

Our platoon, commanded by the same Second Lieutenant who had led us through the arid deserts of North

Africa, had taken up their positions with a fight in mind. He however, had chosen to hide himself in the shadows beneath the bridge, concealed within the tunnel's depths. Above him, the flat expanse of the bridge offered scant comfort, but it was here that a man with a Bren gun lay in wait. His role was clear: to cover us from any threats and shield our positions with the sustained barrage of fire that only a Bren could deliver.

As the night drew its shroud over the battlefield, the steady cadence of the Bren gun was our only assurance that we would not be caught unawares.

CHAPTER 14

THE SECOND TIME DEATH BECKONED

Front Line and the reaper reaches out again.

B Y MID-MORNING, THE TENSION HAD become palpable, thick as the oppressive heat that clung to the battlefield. The silence was punctuated by a voice calling out, "Now come on, Tommy, hand over your guns, and don't try to fight us, just come out of your hole." The menace in the voice was clear, a chilling prelude to the chaos that was about to unfold. Moments later, hand grenades began raining down upon us, their explosions echoing with a ferocity that shattered any sense of calm. The area was filled with a cacophony of blasts and the screams of men caught in the pandemonium.

To my right, just near the edge of the bridge, another pit was now embroiled in its own battle. I glimpsed the Lance

Corporal who manned that position, his face a mask of grim determination as he picked up a grenade. In the same breath, a German soldier entrenched behind a Bren gun sent out a burst of fire, it sliced through the Lance Corporal's right ear, the bullets tearing through flesh with brutal precision, with the same movement his Bren gun moved onto us lying just below him. With a practiced motion the Lance Corporal hurled it towards him. The grenade exploded with a sickening finality, obliterating the enemy and sending a spray of debris into the air. The fuses on the grenades were cruelly short giving precious little time for anything other than sheer reaction.

The Lance Corporal's pain must have been excruciating, yet the man's focus remained unyielding until he had to retreat to the first aid post, located half a mile back. The wound was severe, and he did not return to the fray. If the Lance Corporal hadn't made that fateful throw, within seconds the German soldier perched above us would surely have cut us to pieces.

The scene was grim as we discovered our machine gunner, lifeless with a blade driven deep into his heart. The tension was almost unbearable as we responded to the taunts from the Germans by hurling a grenade in retaliation. To our dismay, the Germans laughed off our feeble attempt, throwing over packets of coarse German tobacco cigarettes. Their mockery was clear—asking if we'd trade some English cigarettes for their offering. Foolishly, some of our men obliged, tossing English cigarettes back across the line.

I couldn't restrain my anger and berated those who had wasted our precious supply. The Germans, undeterred by our dismay, then threw over bunches of flowers with their own dark humour— "Put these on your graves," they taunted, before tossing a few more hand grenades our way. One grenade landed dangerously close to the tunnel where our Lieutenant cowered, and his anguished scream sliced through the chaos, echoing with desperate cries of, "I am wounded!" His voice rang out in a chilling chorus of distress.

Then, amid the turmoil, he commanded, "Fix bayonets, charge!"—a mad and reckless order, expecting us to storm out from our positions. I was in the top hole, the most exposed, and the thought of being the first to charge was foolish. "No way!" I shouted back, "An officer should lead." From the safety of his tunnel, he barked, "Lee, it's you again causing trouble!" I retorted, "You lead and we'll follow!" His response was a pitiful, "I can't, I am wounded," and the reality of his injury—merely a cut above his eyebrow— seemed a far cry from the heroic figure he wished to portray.

Thus, we remained entrenched, immobilized by the absurdity of our predicament, caught between the enemy's mockery and the officer's ineffectual command.

CHAPTER 15

THIRD TIME – THE REAPER MISSES AGAIN

The tough officer shows his true colours.

A S THE SUN BROKE THROUGH the perpetual gloom, it cast a harsh, unfeeling light over our beleaguered position. The heat slowly began to work its magic, steaming and drying our sodden clothes, though it did little to ease the harsh reality of our situation. The two men we had sent to the next mound were nowhere to be seen; they had been captured, a costly reminder of the price of misplaced trust. It was a bitter lesson: when you're in the heart of such chaos, you can't rely on anyone but yourself. The officer, a figure of diminishing authority, had retreated to the first aid post, leaving a gaping hole in our leadership.

With the desperate silence of our predicament settling in, I made my way down the mound to where my mate, Ernie, had dug himself into his own pit. I chose a spot at the bottom of the mound, away from the line of sight, and settled in for a brief respite. As I cracked open a tin of sardines, its pungent aroma mingling with the earthy scent of the field, I was reminded of the simplicity of our sustenance amid the complexity of war. With hard biscuits as my only accompaniment, the meal was a small solace in the midst of the turmoil.

In the chaos of our position, a hedge stretched across the front of the mound, providing a thin veil of cover. From behind it, we crouched, eyes ever-watchful. My moment of relative safety was shattered when the same German sniper, tireless as the dawn, turned his attention toward me once more. But this time, it wasn't a solitary bullet he sent my way—it was a torrent of machine gun fire. The vicious hail of bullets tore through the air, ripping up the mound with lethal accuracy. I dived for cover, my tin of sardines clattering and spilling its contents all over me as I fell into Ernie's pit. For a fleeting moment, I lay there, a stunned reality of our predicament sinking in. The stench of human waste from Ernie's pit mate filled the air.

In the midst of this, I reflected on my narrow escapes. This was the third time I had come dangerously close to death, the fourth if you counted the near-miss in the gun battle me and the Partisans had with the Germans at Salerno. It seemed as if fate, or perhaps divine intervention, was keeping a watchful eye over me. Yet, amidst the lasting barrage of war, there was a brief flicker of reprieve when the sniper's farmhouse was shelled into oblivion. It was the end of his deadly pursuit and a small victory in a world where survival was a fleeting gift.

As dusk began to creep over the battlefield, I was given a

task of some importance: retrieve our section's empty water bottles and journey half a mile back to the farmhouse that served as our headquarters for a fresh supply. With the bottles tied together and slung over my shoulder, I set off, carefully making my way along the hedge and down a narrow path. We were still having trouble with loose Germans, there was a lurking threat of stray Germans. Each bush and shadow could conceal a hidden enemy.

As I advanced cautiously, the tension of the moment was numbing. Suddenly, from within one of the bushes, a figure emerged, causing my heart to leap into my throat. I swung my rifle instinctively, ready to fire, but a voice cut through the din of my fear. "No! Lee, it's me!" The figure was none other than our officer, who had retreated to the first aid post earlier that day.

He looked as though he had been shaken to the core, his eyes wide with fear. He implored me to allow him to accompany me back to the headquarters, pleading for protection. He had been too terrified to return alone, so he had hidden in the bush all day, a pitiful sight compared to the bravado he once boasted in North Africa.

I couldn't help but remind him of his earlier bravado. "Remember what you said back in North Africa? We'd see who was the tough guy at the front line." He winced, acknowledging the truth of my words. "I know," he said, "I apologize. Please, just take me with you."

Grudgingly, I agreed, and he carried the water bottles the rest of the way to the farmhouse, a symbol of his humbled position. Later, it was reported that he was sent back to England and demoted to the rank of an ordinary soldier. It was a fitting outcome, for his cowardice and poor leadership had the potential to cost many lives. Better he faced his shortcomings far from the front lines than endanger the lives of those who faced the real battle.

As I made my way back with the water bottles slung over my shoulder, my nerves were on edge. The weight of the full bottles was a burden, not just physically but mentally as well, for they would hinder my ability to wield my rifle should trouble arise. The path seemed longer and fraught with peril as I carried the heavy load, each step a reminder of the potential danger that lurked in the darkness.

Despite the discomfort and the constant vigilance required, I managed to return safely to our position. The relief on the faces of my comrades was plain to see when they saw the precious water. Each night, the call for water would come from different corners of our makeshift camp. Thirst was a constant companion, and every drop was savoured with gratitude. The bottles, though cumbersome and a hindrance, were a lifeline that kept us going, a small respite in the continuing struggle of war.

The Germans, cunning and ruthless, understood the strategic importance of the bridge we were holding. To dislodge us, they began a relentless assault, launching personnel shells high above our heads. The shells would burst in mid-air, sending a deadly rain of shrapnel cascading down upon us. The very air seemed to hum with the threat of the incoming fragments.

Each day, the battlefield was littered with the wounded—men who had been unlucky enough to catch a piece of that vicious shrapnel. We were forced to huddle low in our makeshift pits, our bodies pressed tightly to the earth, in a desperate bid to avoid the falling debris. The constant tension of waiting for that sharp, searing sting of shrapnel to find its mark was a strain on the nerves, a gnawing anxiety that wore on the spirit. For a fortnight, this grim routine continued, a seemingly endless ordeal of survival against a persistent and merciless enemy.

The man who shared the pit with me was significantly older, in his thirties or more, and he had a tendency to break down in despair, lamenting constantly that he should not be in this hellhole. His incessant whining grated on my nerves, and I warned him bluntly to either quieten down or face being tossed out of the pit. Thankfully, that did the trick, and he fell silent.

But amidst the cacophony of war and the pressure of our dire situation, my own troubles were quietly brewing. The constant crouching and huddling over the days had driven a constant ache into my left knee. What I hadn't realized was that the injury, sustained from being thrown out of the lorry back in England, had been aggravated by the prolonged strain. The damage had worsened, making each movement a bitter reminder of the price of survival.

We had a sergeant among us whose bravery was matched only by his recklessness. Every night, he ventured alone into the darkness, slipping behind enemy lines to gather intelligence on the Germans. His courage was undeniable, but I couldn't help but wonder about his motivation. I asked him once, "Why risk your life each night just to learn where the Germans are?"

His answer was as grim as it was revealing. "I haven't much of a future," he said, "I'm wanted for bigamy back in Britain. If I make it back, I'll face years in prison. So, frankly, I don't give a damn about my life."

One night, he didn't return. That was the end of our sergeant. His absence left a void that no one else was willing to fill. The mound we occupied stretched beyond the bridge and tunnel by a good fifty feet, leaving our right flank exposed. To cover this vulnerability, a guard post was established at the end of the mound, manned with a Bren gun and a stockpile of grenades.

At night, we took turns on guard duty—two hours on, four hours off—while the rest of the section tried to catch what sleep they could. Two men stood watch until dawn, and during the day, the guard was unnecessary. The continual cycle of vigilance was a small price to pay for the safety of our position.

I'd lie prone behind the Brenn gun, my shoulder braced against its weight, ready to unleash a torrent of fire at the first sign of threat. Ernie, my steadfast mate, would hunker down beside me, his fingers never far from the hand grenades that lay within reach. The nights were an unending torrent of cold and dampness, the kind that seeps into your bones and makes every breath a challenge.

Every rustle of a bush, every shadow, every whisper of movement in the dark, had us on edge. I'd murmur to Ernie, "Check that bush, something's moving," and the tension would surge, as if a cold hand had closed around your heart. The knowledge that death could come in a heartbeat sharpened our senses to a razor's edge.

Two hours of this vigilance felt like an eternity. Our watches became the only measure of time, the only promise of relief. When the shift ended and two new men came to replace us, I'd struggle to pry my right hand from the Brenn gun's grip. The weapon, gripped so tightly for so long, seemed to have melded with my flesh. Each movement was a wrench, a reminder of the unrelenting, numbing strain of those nights.

Ernie and I would tumble into the long, narrow pit dug close by, our bodies exhausted and our spirits flagging. We'd pull the groundsheet over us like a shroud, finding a scant comfort in its meagre protection. Once settled, we'd light up a couple of much-needed cigarettes, the smoke curling around us as we savoured the fleeting respite. The smell of tobacco was a luxury we could barely afford, but it was a small solace in the grim reality of our situation.

We were well aware of the danger—if the Germans caught a whiff of our smoke, they'd know we were close, and that would mean trouble. For the entire fortnight, the luxury of a hot meal was a distant memory. Our rations were pitifully simple: Bully beef, hard biscuits, and water, with the occasional tin of sardines thrown in for variety. Each meal was a reminder of the grim conditions we endured, a bleak contrast to the comfort of home we had once taken for granted.

CHAPTER 16

INTO THE LION'S DEN AT SALERNO

**Fodder for the enemy and a
moment of reprieve.**

THE ACHE IN MY LEFT knee had become unbearable. Every time I had to crouch in the pit, it flared up with a vicious intensity. I turned to the man sharing the pit with me and told him to find another spot so I could stretch my leg out and relieve some of the pressure. The pain was non-stop, a constant reminder of the toll this war was taking on my body.

Then, as if by some stroke of fortune, the tanks finally arrived. They rolled into a field behind us, their hulking forms a beacon of hope amidst the desolation. I managed to strike up a conversation with a few of the tank drivers, finding some solace in their presence and the promise of reinforcements.

Just when we thought we'd be granted a little reprieve, we were pulled back from the frontline and marched a couple of miles to a nearby village. We were ready for a rest, for a moment of normality. Instead, we found ourselves marching up and down the main road of the village, a futile exercise meant to keep us occupied. The promise of rest seemed a distant dream, swallowed by the endless march of duty and discomfort.

I limped into the medical officer's tent, the pain in my knee throbbing with each step. I hoped for some relief, some recognition of the agony that had become my constant companion. But what did the man do? He glanced at my swollen joint with the same disinterest one might show to a broken chair, then wrapped a flimsy layer of cotton wool around it. With a dismissive wave, he declared me 'fit for battle' and sent me on my way.

He was a right piece of work, that one. Wrapped in his comfortable surroundings, safe and sound in his medical quarters, he couldn't care less about the suffering of a soldier in the field. To him, I was just another body to be pushed along, regardless of the pain I endured.

A week or two had passed when we assembled to push back into the front line. The endless rain was our only friend, drumming on our gear and soaking through our clothes. I felt the familiar grip of a fever creeping up on me, much like the bronchitis I'd battled in Norfolk the year before. It was a flu-like malaise that seemed to revisit me every so often, and the constant rain only served to worsen it.

I recall us all huddled against a hedge, seeking what little refuge it could offer from the downpour. About twenty feet away, on the other side, the woods loomed dark and foreboding, with a bridge spanning a river like a narrow lifeline.

Our sergeant, a man of unyielding resolve, rounded up my section of eleven men and himself and commanded us to line up, ready to march across the bridge ahead. The shock of his order was striking, as if he'd asked us to walk straight into a storm of lead. "WHAT!" we all exclaimed in disbelief. "We can't do that. There's Germans over there!"

He barked back, "Shut up! Do as you're told, and make as much noise as possible!" It was as if we were sentenced to the electric chair; a grim resignation settled over us. We had no choice but to comply, each step feeling like we were marching straight into a lion's mouth.

We crossed the bridge with a heavy dread, the anticipation of machine gun fire hanging over us like a guillotine. Every step was a countdown to oblivion, and our hearts pounded with the certainty that we'd be torn apart at any moment. We marched on covering the three hundred yards of open ground that had stretched before us, each inch a testament to our courage or folly.

I was stationed at the end, just beside the sergeant. I leaned over and said, "That's far enough. If they were going to open fire, they'd have done it by now." "Ay, that's right," he agreed. Then came the command, "About turn!" And we couldn't march fast enough to escape, our feet pounding back across the bridge, racing toward the safety of our own lines.

To think that the officers in command were willing to gamble with twelve innocent lives, all for the sake of positioning us close to where the Germans were firing from—it's almost unfathomable. As I put pen to paper, the mere recollection makes my heart race anew. It's as though the shadow of that reckless gamble still looms over me, a sombre reminder of the brutal calculus of war where lives are counted as mere pawns.

We retreated behind the hedge, seeking refuge from the rain, and each of us lit up a cigarette, the smoke mingling with the damp, chilly air. I, however, felt too wretched to smoke, and so I requested to see the medical officer. He arrived with his usual air of detached authority, examined my swollen leg with a practiced eye, took my temperature, and inquired about the bandage. I told him who had wrapped it, and to my astonishment, he decreed that I needed forty-eight hours of rest in a camp. It was hard to believe. Next thing I knew, a couple of us were bundled into an American ambulance. The hum of the engine and the bump of the road seemed like a reprieve from the storm, yet the promise of rest felt as distant as a mirage.

We were jolting along a main road when the driver suddenly shouted, "Man, what the hell is happening?" The sky had turned pitch black, a heavy shroud of darkness smothering everything. Vesuvius had erupted in a fury, hurling ash high into the air and spreading it for miles. The road was blanketed with a thick layer of ash, a ghostly reminder of nature's wrath. The driver slammed on the brakes and flicked on the headlights, the beams cutting through the eerie gloom to prevent any other vehicles from blindly colliding with us.

As we prepared to cross the river, we noticed the flames belching from Vesuvius, a fiery spectacle that erupted in a regular rhythm—every three minutes. It was a fearsome sight, the volcano's rage a crisp contrast to our own small troubles.

We finally reached a muddy field designated as a 'rest area,' a scant three miles from the front line. Another soldier and I set up in a two-man 'bivouac,' a modest shelter that offered a semblance of normality. He was a good fellow, and we were treated to decent food—something of a luxury, and as much as we wanted. It felt like a small, hard-earned victory, a chance to savour a fleeting moment of solace amid the turmoil.

In the stillness of the tent, while the world outside seemed to drift into the murky haze of war, I found myself alone during the day. The weight of impending return to the front line hung heavy on my shoulders, a gnawing dread that refused to be silenced. With a fervent desperation, I began to pray to Our Lady, pleading for her protection, begging her to spare me from the cruel fate that loomed before me.

And then, in the midst of that fervent prayer, an extraordinary vision unfolded. Before my eyes, as if conjured from the very fabric of my faith, I swear I saw an image of her, resplendent and serene, appearing in the dim confines of the tent. The vision was fleeting, yet it left an indelible mark upon my soul. I was left in a daze, questioning the reality of what I had seen, my mind struggling to reconcile the divine with the harshness of the world around me.

I was not under the influence of any medication, nor had I indulged in anything that might distort my senses. The vision remained with me, a hauntingly beautiful memory that defied logic and reason, but which I would carry with me always. In that moment, it was as if the divine had reached out from the darkness to offer a glimmer of hope amidst the despair.

In the midst of the squalor and strain of camp life, an Italian photographer appeared, moving through the encampment with a sense of casual authority. His presence, marked by the click of his camera and the air of nostalgia he carried with him, was a rare distraction from the grind of our existence.

One of my comrades, sharing the same tent and a similar sense of weariness, seized the opportunity. We approached the photographer, our pockets decidedly lighter than the weight of our burdens. With not enough money to afford separate portraits and a joint one together we decided to have our likeness captured together and cut it in half to provide the individual portrait.

The photographer snapped a single, well-composed shot of the two of us, side by side—a fleeting moment of camaraderie amid the endless march of war. We had three copies made. Once the photographs were developed, we carefully cut one down the middle.

Even now, years later, those two photographs remain with me. They are more than just pieces of paper; they are relics of a time when we sought a semblance of normality and connection, a reminder of the bonds formed and the fleeting joys.

At rest camp for 48 hours. Three miles from the front line.

CHAPTER 17

THE FRONTLINE, OR THE ILLUSION OF IT

Return to the battle and divine intervention.

THE SUN HUNG HIGH AND fierce as a jeep roared up, dust swirling in its wake. It was a brief respite from the dogged pace of war, but it was time to return to the fray. I climbed in with a fellow from our unit, and we were whisked off, dropped a half-mile from the front lines. The driver's urgency was palpable; he left us in a cloud of dust, eager to distance himself from the danger, as the menace of incoming shells was ever-present.

As we trudged down the road towards the clamour of battle, a jeep sped towards us, tearing up the dirt and gravel. In the front sat a brigadier, his face etched with tension and grim determination. He slammed the brakes and shouted, "Where the hell do you think you're going?"

We explained our situation: a short-lived forty-eight-hour rest and our need to report to the nearest field hospital before rejoining our unit. The brigadier's eyes flared with urgency. "Forget the field hospital! Get back to the front line immediately—the Germans are breaking through our defences!"

His haste was as clear as the fear in his voice. It was no surprise that he was fleeing the scene with such desperation. The chap with me had a gaping hole in his leg, the result of a nasty abscess. I glanced at him and then back at the brigadier's retreating jeep.

"Don't mind that brigadier," I said firmly. "We'll head to the field hospital on this road as we were instructed to do and sort ourselves out before we rejoin the fight."

In the midst of chaos, sometimes the battlefield's demands had to be balanced with the need to mend and ready oneself for the next clash.

I limped into the field hospital and reported to the medical officer. He gave me a cursory look, then examined the bandage on my knee, his fingers gently prodding at the swelling. "Is it painful?" he asked, without looking up.

"Like hell," I replied. "It locks up sometimes, and when it does, it's murder."

He sighed, straightening up. "You'll have to go back to No. 2 Field Hospital. I can't treat this here, and it's too dangerous for you to return to the front line. If your knee locks up there, you'll be a burden to your unit."

I nodded, feeling a surge of relief deep within me. His words were a godsend. I couldn't imagine the horrors of hobbling through the front lines with a leg that could seize up at any moment. "Thank God and his blessed mother," I muttered under my breath.

The other chap wasn't as lucky. The officer gave him the go-ahead to return to his unit. I saw the defeated look in his eyes as he packed up, his leg wound still fresh and festering. I watched him walk down that horror-laden road, alone, heading back into the nightmare we had both been spared from—for now. I wished I could have done something more, but war had a way of turning even the best of us into mere survivors, doing what we could to stay alive.

The ambulance bounced along the uneven road, heading away from the front line, and I felt the tension leave my body, inch by inch. As I settled into my seat, my eyes drifted over the other men inside. Right across from me, sitting rigid with his hand bandaged, was a familiar face from my section.

"What's happened to you?" I asked, my voice low.

He glanced up, eyes hollow, then muttered, "Cleaning my rifle. It went off. Took three fingers off my left hand." His words were clipped, forced, as if he didn't quite believe the lie himself.

I nodded, though I knew better. We'd all thought about it—Ernie and I had talked about the ways we could get out of the nightmare. "What if we shoot each other in the calf muscle?" we'd joked, as if it was some kind of solution. Then we debated the possibility of throwing a foot under a tank's treads. It was always a half-joke, half-serious. But something had to snap inside a man to actually do it. To push yourself over that line from fear to desperation.

This young soldier had crossed it. He couldn't bear the thought of going back to the front, especially with the

Germans breaking through. His rifle hadn't just gone off—it was no accident. I stared at his bandaged hand, and I knew he'd chosen a way out, a path lined with self-inflicted pain.

But the price for that moment of escape was steep. He'd traded three fingers for a few years in a military prison. Self-inflicted wounds in the face of the enemy meant you were branded a coward. There'd be no sympathy, no understanding—just cold, hard judgment from the top brass.

I looked out the ambulance window, the barren landscape rushing by. In this war, we were all on the edge, some of us closer to falling off than others. But he had chosen his fate, and in a way, I couldn't blame him.

The orderly returned with a roll of Elastoplast, and they wound it around my knee, securing it firm. For the first time in weeks, I felt the joint steady itself. The pain was still there, but less intense, like a storm that had passed its peak.

"There," the doctor said, stepping back, wiping his hands. "You'll be able to move on to No. 3 Field Hospital, and then on to No. 4 after that."

I blinked at him, barely comprehending. Was this really happening? I'd expected the usual brush-off, another forced march back to the front. But no—this felt like a miracle. A reprieve, as if the gods of war had finally decided to look the other way.

As they handed me back my medical records, I saw something scrawled in the corner—*I D K*. My heart sank.

"I D K?" I asked, half-joking. "Does that mean 'I don't know'?"

The doctor gave me a weary look, barely amused. "It

means 'Invalided Down the Line,' soldier. You're out of the front for now."

I nodded, feeling relief wash over me. Invalided down the line. The words were a gift, one I would not take lightly. For the first time in months, I was being sent back, away from the horror of the front line, away from the endless rain of bullets and the shriek of artillery.

After a few more days and another long, bone-jarring ride through the war-torn countryside, I finally arrived at No. 4 Field Hospital. This was the last stop before leaving the front for good, and the sense of relief among the men was undeniable. You could see it in their eyes, a flicker of hope where there had only been exhaustion and fear.

As we filed through the hospital's intake, stretchers were lined up, waiting to ferry the wounded from here to the next stage of the journey. I was aching all over but still on my feet. I told the orderly, "I'd rather try and walk."

He shook his head, barely listening, as if he'd heard the same request a hundred times before. "Not allowed," he said flatly, gesturing for me to lie down.

I hesitated, but the prospect of being sent back to the front because I'd defied orders wasn't something I was willing to risk. Reluctantly, I climbed onto the stretcher, the cool canvas sagging beneath my weight.

The ambulance ride was rough, every bump and jolt sending new waves of pain through my knee, but it didn't matter now. The front line was behind me. Ahead lay Naples and, beyond that, the sea.

We finally rolled into the docks at Naples, the salt air mingling with the smell of fuel and sweat. There, moored alongside the pier, was the *La Vita*, a hulking, captured

Italian hospital ship. She was an old vessel, battle-scarred and weather-beaten, but she might as well have been the finest liner in the world for what she promised: a ticket home, or at least to safety.

There must have been a couple of hundred casualties onboard already, men from every corner of the battlefield, some bandaged head to toe, others barely conscious. We were carried up the gangplank in silence, the soft lap of the sea against the hull the only sound cutting through the tension. I caught a glimpse of the horizon beyond the ship, an endless stretch of blue water that led away from this place of death and destruction.

The ship pitched and rolled beneath us, cutting through the slate-grey waves with the defiance of a beast that refused to succumb to the sea's fury. It had been days since we left the relative safety of Naples, and the men below deck were growing restless. Whispers began to drift like the smoke of our last cigarettes—rumours that we were bound for Blighty, the motherland. The prospect of returning home, even for a fleeting breath, lifted their spirits.

But I knew better. The sea wasn't our ally in this war, and neither was fortune.

Days into our voyage, with the wind howling like a jackal and the rain pounding the deck in sheets, the truth finally hit us. We weren't heading for the cool shores of England. Instead, Algiers loomed on the horizon like a mirage, shimmering in the distance through the downpour.

It was the first week of December, 1943, and the wet season was in full fury. The rain came down in torrents, as if the heavens had conspired to wash us from the earth, we eventually made land.

I found myself in a hospital in Algiers in the last bed of a long row, tucked right next to the flap of a large marquee. The canvas walls flapped occasionally in the wind, and through the gaps, I could see the sprawling mass of the hospital grounds, a patchwork of tents and makeshift wards that stretched as far as the eye could see.

I was the only British soldier in that marquee, the rest were a mix of Yanks and Canadians. It wasn't surprising, really—this was the 46th Canadian Division attached to the Fifth American Army, slogging it out through the mud and blood of Italy. Most of them had been fighting alongside us, but you could always tell a Canadian by his voice, and the Yanks, well, they stood out with their endless chatter.

I lay there, listening to them. They were swapping stories the kind of stories soldiers tell to take their minds off the pain. They were laughing about their time in Cardiff, of all places. Cardiff! It seemed absurd to me, lying in a war zone so far from home that they'd be talking about the joys of a leave spent in a Welsh port city. But there they were, going on about the pubs, the girls, and how much fun they'd had.

"Man, Cardiff was something else," one of the Yanks said, his voice full of nostalgia. "You could drink all night and still have enough left in your pocket for breakfast."

"Yeah, and the girls weren't shy, either," one of the Canadians chimed in, drawing a round of laughter from the others.

I turned over in my bed, staring at the canvas above me, feeling a strange sense of isolation. Their voices drifted on, filling the tent with the kind of carefree talk that seemed miles removed from the war outside. Cardiff—home felt so far away, even though it was just across the sea. I hadn't been back in years, not since before this whole bloody mess started.

As I listened to them go on, I couldn't help but feel a pang of longing. They spoke about it like it was some distant paradise, untouched by the horrors we had seen. But I knew better. It was just another place, another stop before the next battle, just like everything else.

On the 12th of December, 1943, I turned 21. Some birthday that was. No fanfare, no cake, not even a mate nearby to share a cigarette with. Just another day in the middle of a war. I lay there, half-dozing in my cot, surrounded by the chatter of Yanks and Canadians, none of whom knew or cared about my birthday. I could've been a ghost for all the difference it made.

The air inside the tent was thick with the smell of damp canvas and the stale odour of sweat and antiseptic. Outside, the wind whipped through the hospital camp, carrying with it the distant rumble of artillery fire. It was a strange thing, really—turning 21. Back home, it might have meant something. A man's age, a moment to be marked with a pint at the pub, a toast to the future. But here, in the middle of this bloody war, it was just another day of survival.

Suddenly, a little Arab boy stuck his head under the tent flap, his dark eyes wide and curious. He grinned, flashing white teeth, and said, "You buy dates?"

I looked at him, half-amused and half-annoyed. I didn't have a penny to my name, not that it mattered out here. But the lad was persistent, holding up a small box of dates like it was treasure.

"No money," I said, waving him off.

He squinted at me, then pointed to the small bar of soap

I had on the table next to my bed. The last luxury I had. He wanted to trade. Soap for dates. I hesitated for a second, but then thought, why the hell not?

"Alright," I muttered, tossing the soap to him. His grin grew wider as he placed the box of dates in my hand and scampered off before I could change my mind.

I sat there for a moment, staring at the dates in my hand. They weren't much—a small, scrappy box of Algerian dates. But I couldn't help but chuckle to myself. Happy 21st birthday, Billy. No party, no friends, no fanfare—just you and a box of dates. I popped one in my mouth, tasting the sticky sweetness on my tongue. It wasn't much, but it was something.

And in that small moment, with the wind howling outside and the sound of distant guns reminding me where I was, I celebrated in my own quiet way.

After about a week, I found myself in the orthopaedic ward, surrounded by men whose bodies had been twisted and torn by the brutality of war. We were all waiting for the knife, each of us nursing injuries that told stories of survival, and some of them, of sheer luck. My knee throbbed with a dull ache, a constant reminder that I wasn't far from being sent back into the fray if I didn't make a decision soon.

I knew I had the right to refuse the operation, and it weighed heavily on my mind. This wasn't some run-of-the-mill cartilage repair—they'd told me as much. No, this was going to be a deep cut, through bone and ligament. The words "no guarantee" had been thrown around too often for my liking, and I wasn't the kind of man who put much faith in hope alone.

There was no assurance that my knee wouldn't be

permanently stiff afterward, a stiff leg that could cripple me for life, or worse—make me a burden in battle if I ever returned. They'd handed me a release form to sign, some official nonsense that would place the outcome of the surgery squarely on my shoulders. As if that didn't already weigh enough.

And then there was that mysterious 'I D K'—it really meant Internal Dislocation Knee. That's what they called it, but what lay beneath the skin was anyone's guess. They could open me up and find a mess of bone and tendon that even their best surgeons couldn't fix. Or they could patch me up just enough to send me back to the front lines. Either way, the stakes were high, and it was my decision to make.

I lay there, listening to the moans and snores of the men around me, each of them facing their own battle on those iron beds. War doesn't stop at the front line—it follows you into the hospitals, the recovery wards, into the deepest recesses of your mind. The scars are just as deep inside as they are on the body.

As I stared at the ceiling, I weighed my options. Refuse the surgery and live with the pain and uncertainty, or take the gamble and risk coming out worse than before. It was the kind of choice no man should have to make, but here I was, in a world where decisions like these were all too common.

In the end, I knew what I had to do.

After a couple of days in the ward, things settled into a grim routine. The surgeon would make his rounds, accompanied by his retinue of junior doctors and orderlies, all of them shuffling from bed to bed, reviewing charts and making decisions like gods passing judgement. When they finally reached my bed, the surgeon—a tall, stiff man with a haughty air—picked up my chart, glanced at it briefly, then spoke as if he were ordering a meal, "Get that man ready for surgery."

I could feel the eyes of the others in the ward on me. Surgery was a final step for most of them—an irreversible one. As they started to walk away, something stirred deep inside me, a defiance that had been forged on the battlefield, tempered in the mud and blood of war.

"Excuse me, sir," I called out.

The surgeon stopped in his tracks and turned slowly, fixing me with a cold, dismissive gaze. He looked down his nose at me as though I was a bothersome fly in his operating theatre. "Yes, what do you want?" he asked, his tone more bored than curious.

I met his gaze and didn't blink. "Can you guarantee that I will not have a stiff leg after you've operated on my knee?"

A flicker of irritation crossed his face. "What?" he said, incredulous, as if I'd just asked him to perform magic. "Of course I can't. I don't know what will happen afterwards."

That was all I needed to hear. I wasn't some fresh recruit who'd bend at the first sign of authority. I had survived through sheer will, facing death more times than I could count. "Well," I said, my voice steady as stone, "in that case, I'm not going to have it done."

For a moment, the entire ward went silent. Every patient, every orderly, every doctor stood frozen, wide-eyed and open-mouthed, as though I'd just declared war on the surgeon himself. The surgeon's eyes narrowed, his face flushed with anger and disbelief. "What did you say?"

he barked, his voice rising, a ripple of authority cracking through the tent.

"I said," I repeated calmly, "I'm not going to have it done."

He stared at me as if I had just committed the ultimate act of insubordination. To him, a man like me—a soldier, a casualty of war—wasn't supposed to question a decision like this. But the last thing I was afraid of was this pompous surgeon. I had been through hell, and his sterile world of scalpels and charts didn't intimidate me in the least.

"You don't understand," he growled, stepping closer. "This is your best chance."

"No," I said, matching his gaze without flinching. "I think I understand perfectly. But I've survived too much to take a gamble with my leg. If you can't guarantee I'll Walk out of here without a stiff leg, I won't risk it."

For a moment, we gazed at each other locked in a silent battle of wills then I lay back in my bed, heart still pounding, but a calm certainty washed over me. I'd made my choice. I'd fought too hard and come too far to let some stranger in a white coat decide my fate.

The surgeon's face turned a shade of red I hadn't seen before, his outrage spilling over like a dam breaking. He whirled on the orderly beside him, the veins in his neck pulsing with fury. "Get that man out of here!" he bellowed, his voice echoing across the ward like a gunshot. Then, without another word, he turned on his heel, his entourage trailing behind him like confused ducklings. They were astonished, their faces still marked with disbelief as they followed their master out of the ward his pride wounded far more than any patient under his care.

The orderly, a young man with wide eyes and a nervous twitch, bent down toward me as if I were a dangerous animal he didn't want to provoke. "I've never heard anyone speak to him like that," he whispered, clearly still stunned. "He's Sir something-or-other—famous orthopaedic surgeon. People wait months to get in front of him. You, well... you just told him to get lost."

I shrugged, swinging my legs out of the bed, the weight of it all finally starting to sink in. "He might be some big name around here," I said, reaching for my boots, "but I've met a lot of men who thought they were invincible. They all bled the same in the end."

The orderly was still gawking, his mouth slightly open as if he couldn't quite believe what had just transpired. He glanced toward the door where Sir Something-or-other had disappeared, then back to me, as if I'd sprouted a second head. "Well, I suppose you'll be moving wards then."

"Seems that way," I said, pulling my shirt over my shoulders. My knee twinged with pain, but I ignored it. Pain was an old companion now and one I could handle better than blind obedience.

The orderly led me through the bustling corridors, the faint smell of antiseptic in the air, nurses and doctors moving like ants, everyone with a purpose. As we walked, I couldn't help but notice how different I felt from the rest of them, how out of place. They hadn't seen what I'd seen, hadn't faced death with the barrel of a gun pointed at them. These men and women stitched people back together, but they didn't understand what it meant to truly fight for survival.

We reached another ward, quieter, with fewer patients. The orderly handed me a bundle of my clothes, looking at me once more as if he were about to say something but thought better of it. "Good luck," he muttered, before turning and hurrying away, no doubt eager to get back to the safety of his routines.

I stood there for a moment, taking in the stillness of the room. I hadn't had the operation, and for now, I was still walking on my own two feet. That was good enough for me. But I knew, as I looked at the rows of beds and the empty faces of the men lying in them, that this wasn't the end of the battle. There would always be more to fight—whether it was on the front lines, in a hospital ward, or in the trenches of my own mind.

And as long as I could stand, I'd fight on.

CHAPTER 18

LIGHT AFTER DARKNESS – CHRISTMAS HOPE

In the midst of chaos, a fleeting moment of joy and camaraderie

A WEEK OR SO AFTER THE surgeon's scolding and my transfer to another ward, I found myself standing before two medical officers. The room was cold, sterile, and entirely impersonal—a far cry from the chaos and blood I'd left behind on the front lines. The officers, stiff-backed and unsmiling, barely glanced up from their charts. It was as though my fate was already written before I'd even opened my mouth.

They called out my name and asked a few curt questions about my knee, glancing at me only occasionally as if I were an animal being evaluated for slaughter. But none of that mattered, not as much as the grading they would assign me. A1 meant fit for duty—fit to march back into the jaws of hell. B7 meant a reprieve, a chance at life away from the front lines, away from the bullets and the blood. When they finally handed down their judgment, I exhaled in sheer relief: B7. No more infantry, no more front lines. Thank God, my prayers had been answered.

It felt like I had cheated death, yet again. What awaited me now was nothing short of a miracle.

Soon after, I was transferred to the Royal Army Service Corps (RASC), a quiet backwater compared to the horrors I had left behind. My new posting was a petrol serving company, far removed from the gunfire and shrieking shells of the front. We were based just outside of Algiers, in a small, sun-baked Arab village called Hamen Lif. It was a dusty place, with the heat of North Africa pressing down on us like a suffocating blanket. But compared to where I'd been, it was paradise.

My job was simple but essential: filling five-gallon jerry cans with petrol, which were then loaded onto lorries and tanks heading back into the heart of battle. There was no glory here, but there was peace, and that was enough for me. The sweat would pour from us in rivers under the punishing sun, the stench of petrol always in our nostrils. But for all the discomfort, I couldn't help but feel grateful for the mundanity of it.

I learned to acetylene weld, a skill I'd never imagined picking up in a war zone. Whenever one of the petrol cans leaked, I'd be called over to patch it up, bending low over the glowing metal, the heat from the welding torch mixing with the sweltering desert air. It wasn't glamorous work by any stretch, but it was a job that kept me off my feet and away from danger. Sitting down, covered in sweat and soot,

Algiers 1944

my fingers clumsy with the heavy torch, I felt something I hadn't felt in a long time—safety.

The days blurred together under that fierce African sun. There was always petrol to fill, cans to patch, and lorries to send off. And though the heat was nearly unbearable, it beat the freezing mud and blood-soaked fields of Italy any day. We'd sit around in the evenings, my fellow soldiers and I, swapping stories and wondering how much longer the war would drag on. We were so far removed from the fight that it almost felt like we were part of another world altogether. A quieter one, where the only battles were with the heat and the smell of petrol.

Looking back, it felt like fate had steered me here, to this tiny village outside of Algiers, where the war was just a distant roar. But I knew, deep down, that none of us were truly safe—not until the last bullet was fired and the last man was sent home.

The day the Sahara wind swept in the heat was unbearable—like stepping into an inferno with the oven door wide open. The sky, once a deep, unblemished blue, turned hazy as millions of locusts filled the air. They surged like a living storm, their dark bodies swirling in the hot wind. The air crackled with their constant droning, an incessant buzz that seemed to echo the turmoil of the war.

The Arabs, ever resourceful, took advantage of the locust plague. They moved swiftly among the swarms, scooping the insects into baskets and bags with practiced ease. These hardy souls would take their catch home to fry and eat, a grim reminder of survival in a land where every resource was a precious commodity. It was a sight both repulsive and fascinating, a testament to the resilience of life in such harsh conditions.

I spent about six months in that blistering environment, surrounded by the unmerciful heat and the ever-present threat of locusts. It was an odd juxtaposition—amongst the heat and the dust, I found a strange solace in the routine of the RASC. It was a welcome respite from the chaos of the front lines, especially given the ongoing battles in northern Italy and Austria. My work was steady, and for once, the threat of enemy fire seemed a distant echo.

Eventually, the time came for me to move on. I was transferred from the petrol unit to a bulk supply depot situated just outside Naples. The transition was a welcome one. Naples, with its lush landscapes and more temperate climate, offered a stark contrast to the searing heat of the Sahara. The depot was a hub of activity, a crucial point for the distribution of supplies to the various fronts, and I found the work both demanding and satisfying.

Before settling into my new role at the depot, I was stationed briefly at a transit camp. It was a temporary haven for soldiers like me, a place where men from all branches of the army—infantry, artillery, and more—mingled in a kind of limbo. The camp was a melting pot of different uniforms and stories, each soldier waiting for his next assignment, his next destination. Here, we exchanged tales of the front lines and the peculiarities of the places we had been, the camaraderie providing a fleeting escape from the reality of war.

The transit camp, though far from the action, was alive with a different kind of energy—a waiting game filled with

Algiers 1944

uncertainty and hope. It was in these moments, amid the hustle and the endless shuffle of men, that I felt a mixture of relief and restlessness, knowing that while the immediate danger was behind me, the war still raged on, claiming its toll in distant lands.

Then came Christmas Day, a momentary reprieve from the ruthless grind of war. On this day our meals were served in a grand, canvas marquee

that had been transformed for the occasion. Christmas was one of those rare days when tradition took precedence over protocol, and this year, the officers of the Black Watch— hardy and formidable infantrymen—were tasked with serving the Christmas dinner.

The meal was a grand affair, a rare treat amidst the rigors of wartime. The aroma of roast beef and Christmas pudding filled the air, a welcome distraction from the usual fare of field rations. The top officer, a towering Scotsman with a bristling black moustache, made his rounds with a group of younger officers. His presence was commanding, his eyes sharp as he asked each table if anyone wanted more.

Ordinarily, one wouldn't dare ask for seconds, but this day was different. When he reached our table, I seized the opportunity. I stood up and with a mix of boldness and hunger said, "Yes, thank you, I'd like some more."

The Scotsman's gaze dropped to me, his imposing figure casting a long shadow. "What was that, soldier?" he demanded, his voice as stern as the Highland winds. I repeated my request, unwavering.

He turned to the Sergeant Major, his face a mask of barely contained irritation. "Did you hear what this man said?"

The Sergeant Major's eyes bore into me, a blend of disbelief and disapproval. "You've had your rations allotted to you, and you have the cheek to ask for more? Do you realize there are men up at the front line who have nothing to eat today?"

Without missing a beat, I replied, "I know. I've been up there. How about you?"

The Sergeant Major's eyes widened slightly, but it was Christmas and the usual strictness of military discipline was softened by the spirit of the holiday. The confrontation, charged with tension, was met with a begrudging tolerance. The Black Watch officers, recognizing the irony and the truth in my words, allowed the matter to pass without further rebuke.

So, amidst the roast beef and the Christmas pudding, I found a small victory in my defiance. It was a fleeting moment of rebellion, a reminder of the complexities of duty and the thin line between respect and rebellion. And as I enjoyed the extra helping, I couldn't help but reflect on the strange, bittersweet nature of Christmas at the front, where even the simplest joys were tinged with the shadows of conflict.

From the Transit camp I was dispatched to the bulk supply depot where ships from Naples dock unloaded their precious cargo. The depot buzzed with the frenetic energy of sorting and distribution. We were the linchpin in the supply chain, ensuring that the rations from the dock made their way to the troop units scattered across the region.

Amidst the bustling activity, I crossed paths with a fellow named Ernie Turner, hailing from the windswept moors of Ilkley in Yorkshire. Ernie and I forged a solid friendship, a bond that endured until he was finally demobilized and sent back home. Our days together were a welcome distraction from the bitter truth of war.

Taken in Naples 1944

Our duties took us to places like Padua and Verona, though, in the haze of time, those cities blurred into the backdrop of our war-torn existence. What stands clear in my memory is a visit to Naples with Ernie and another mate. We made our way to King Victor Emmanuel's Palace (The Royal Palace of Naples), a grand structure with around seventy steps leading up to its imposing entrance.

The palace had been transformed into a NAAFI (Navy, Army and Air Force Institute, an organisation that provides recreational facilities to British military personnel) canteen, and inside it was nothing short of magnificent. The vast expanse of its interior, with rooms that spoke of opulence and grandeur, was a pleasant contrast to the rigors of our daily grind. It was a rare moment of luxury amidst the harshness of war, a reminder of the world beyond the conflict, and a brief respite that allowed us to momentarily escape the relentless demands of our duty.

Just before we entered the grandiose expanse of King Emmanuel's Palace, I spotted an Interflora flower shop nestled outside, its modest sign a beacon of normality amid the chaos. On an impulse that felt both indulgent and necessary, I decided to order a grand spray of flowers—a bouquet so lavish it set me back a full month's pay. This extravagant gesture was intended for a special occasion: my mother's birthday, January 1st, 1944.

Months later, when I finally returned home on leave, Sheila, my sister, recounted the story of that delivery. The Interflora man had knocked on the door of our home with the bouquet in hand. My mother, initially bewildered, had protested that such a splendid arrangement couldn't possibly be for her. It wasn't until she read the note attached— "From your loving son, Bill"—that the truth dawned. Sheila, brimming with excitement, paraded the flowers around the neighbourhood, a token of pride and affection that lit up our home in the midst of the war's shadow.

That moment, etched into my memory, was a small victory amidst the hardships, a testament to the bond between mother and son that the war could not diminish.

My mother must have felt a surge of pride, her heart warmed by the thoughtfulness of her son even as the world outside was consumed by conflict.

She often sent me two hundred Woodbines through an organization like the Salvation Army, which seemed to be everywhere, considering how scattered the troops were. My mother would pay for them 'Duty Free,' which made them considerably cheaper, though the expense was still a burden she could ill afford. Her letters came regularly, and I often wished I had kept them. My sister, Mag, also wrote to me. There was a profound comfort in receiving those letters, in reading about the family's news from home. My mother insisted on receiving a photo of me every so often, a tangible proof of my well-being, for she missed us all terribly. That's why I still have a few photos of myself abroad in uniform; they were her lifeline to the world I had become a part of.

I spent about six months in that unit before I had the chance to visit my brother Tom, who was stationed at a monastery in a place called Castel-Del-Mare. *(Castellammare di Stabia is situated on the Bay of Naples about 30 km (19 mi) southeast of Naples, on the route to Sorrento.)* I was granted leave to stay at his billet for a weekend. Tom was with the Signal Corps, and his post was not far along the coast from Naples. It was a rare and welcome break from the hard grind of military life, a brief return to normality.

CHAPTER 19

THE WAR ENDS – FROM VERONA TO VIENNA

Journey Through New Lands: The Yankee's Folly and the Shadow of Captivity

T HE NEXT TOWNS I FOUND myself in were Verona and Padua, places where history seemed to seep from every cobblestone. We pushed north forcing the Germans out of Italy. Our task was clear: keep the supply lines open and ensure the troops were well-fed and equipped as we drove the Germans out. It was punishing work, but the sights of Italy provided some solace.

From there, I was transferred to Genoa. This was Italy's most important port and with its heavy industry had been a prime target being constantly bombarded by the allies from sea and air. The city endured 86 air raids, of which 51 occurred in 1944. I was stationed at what I believe was the thirty-eighth Bulk Supply Depot (B.S.D.). Genoa was

Taken in Genoa in 1945

a different world altogether. Amidst the rugged beauty of the Ligurian coast, I found a strange kind of peace. One of the perks was having access to Mussolini's old swimming pool—a grand relic of his era. I spent many afternoons in that pool, swimming laps and trying to forget the wars that raged outside. I was stationed in Genoa for about twelve months, and throughout it all, Ernie Turner remained by my side. Our bond, forged in these still turbulent times.

The war, at long last, came to an end in May 1945. The thunder of artillery and the crack of rifles had finally fallen silent, leaving behind a strange, almost eerie quiet. We were soldiers no longer bound by the brutal rhythm of battle, but by the slow, uncertain return to a life we had nearly forgotten.

Then came the transfer to a charming little village named Appiano, nestled near the foothills of the Italian Alps. It was as though time had stood still in this place, untouched by the violence that had ravaged Europe. The air was crisp, and the mountains loomed like ancient sentinels, their peaks dusted in pure white snow, sparkling beneath the early morning sun.

Appiano seemed like a world apart, with its cobbled streets, the slow clinking of cowbells from nearby pastures, and the warm, earthy scent of pine forests that surrounded us. It was a place where the war felt distant, almost like a forgotten nightmare, though its shadows lingered in the corners of our minds.

As we settled into this newfound peace, it felt surreal—almost as if we had stepped into a story yet to be written, with the next chapter unknown. But here, in the heart of the Alps, there was a sense of renewal. Life had returned to the land, and, for the first time in years, hope was no longer just a word whispered in the trenches, but something tangible, something real.

Appiano was a place where we could, if only for a moment, imagine that the horrors of the past had not left permanent scars on our souls. But deep down, we all knew that even in the most beautiful of places, history had a way of lingering. And though the guns were quiet, the memories of war were far from gone.

The snow here was a different breed altogether—crisp and clean, untouched by the slushy mess that plagued lower altitudes. It was in this serene setting that I experienced a slice of unspoiled beauty.

One day, I managed to borrow a car from a corporal, he had taken it from a German soldier—such an odd twist of fate in those chaotic times. With Ernie by my side, I took the car up into the mountains, climbing through the deep snow that blanketed the slopes. At the summit, we found a quaint bar, its warmth inviting after the chill of the climb. We enjoyed a couple of glasses of wine, toasting to our unexpected adventure.

As we sipped our drinks, it became clear to us that we were likely the first British soldiers to have ventured this far. The locals' unease was palpable, though they didn't voice it directly. Their glances said it all: they seemed wary of us, as if our presence alone was enough to stir the ghosts of recent battles.

We knew we had to make our descent before darkness fell, for the narrow mountain road was cloaked in snow, and navigating it in the dark could be perilous. As we began our journey down, Ernie, ever keen to share the driving, asked if he could take the wheel. I agreed, given that it was all downhill from there.

The road twisted and turned, and we were making good progress until we approached a particularly sharp bend. Without warning, the car skidded, and we found ourselves sliding uncontrollably towards the edge. I scrambled to correct the steering, my heart pounding as the edge loomed closer. Fortune was on our side that day—the car's bumper collided with a mile-stone, jolting us back onto the road and into a deep snow drift.

We spent what felt like an age digging the car out, our hands numb from the cold. The effort was worth it, though, and we eventually managed to free the vehicle and make our way back to the billets.

As the days passed, the inevitable happened. Ernie was demobbed, and just like that, he was gone. It felt like the end of an era—one that had been marked by camaraderie and shared trials.

Whilst stationed at Appiano in Italy, a few of us were taken up into the mountains, to a ski resort near Bolzano. It was a world apart from the mud, blood, and grime we'd lived through during the war. The place was buzzing with skiers from all corners of the globe, dressed in the finest gear, laughing, their faces flushed with the thrill of the slopes and the cold mountain air. We felt like outsiders, intruders in a world that didn't belong to us anymore.

We decided to give skiing a try. There was a small hill nearby, nothing too ambitious, but enough to show us just how out of place we were. I strapped on the skis, feeling the awkward weight of them beneath me, and set off down the slope. Within moments, I lost all control, tumbling headfirst into the snow. It was ridiculous, really—one moment a soldier, the next a fool buried in a snowdrift. The others didn't fare much better, and soon we were all laughing at ourselves, but there was something bitter in it, a reminder of how far removed we were from the carefree skiers who swarmed the resort.

Afterwards, we tried to get into one of the bars for a drink, but the crowds inside were thick, and the prices were beyond anything we could afford. It astounded me to see all these people—well-heeled, relaxed, enjoying themselves so soon after the war. Only the rich could indulge in this kind of luxury, while the rest of us were still in uniform, still bound to duty, still part of an occupying force.

As we trudged back to our base at Appiano that evening, we couldn't shake the feeling of dejection. Those rich people would carry on skiing, drinking their fine wine, and eating lavish meals while we watched from outside, eating our cold sandwiches, soldiers in name, but with no sense of victory in our hearts. It was clear—the war may have ended, but the divide between those who suffered and those who stood untouched remained as deep as ever.

On another occasion, I found myself in desperate need of a dentist. The nearest one was about ten miles away, in a hospital still run by the German Army. It was a strange reality—we were the victors, but here I was, relying on the enemy for a simple tooth extraction. My officer in charge gave me the order to take a small German Volkswagen that had belonged to a few German POW officers in our camp. Naturally, when I went to inform them, they kicked up a fuss, protesting that the car was still theirs in spirit, if not in possession. I stood my ground and told them firmly that I'd be taking the car at a specific time tomorrow, whether they liked it or not.

The next day, I collected the car with a German soldier as my passenger, and off we went to the hospital. The trip there was uneventful, aside from the eerie sensation of driving a car that had once carried the enemy through these same streets, the seats worn in by German officers who'd never imagined they would lose. It was on the way back that trouble hit. I was halfway between the hospital and camp when the gear lever snapped clean off at the base, leaving only an inch of metal sticking out, utterly useless for shifting gears. I cursed the Germans for what had obviously been sabotage—those officers must have hack-sawed the lever in some petty act of defiance, hoping it would cripple their own car, now that it was in our hands.

There I was, stuck miles from anywhere, with no way to properly use the gears. It was a grim situation, but I wasn't about to let a little piece of metal defeat me. I jammed my palm against the inch of lever that was left, forcing it into second gear. That was all I could manage, and it meant I'd have to drive the rest of the way in second, the engine roaring and straining as I pushed it beyond what it was built for. By the time I reached camp, the car sounded like it was about to fall apart, but I made it.

The German officers, smugly pretending innocence, had the nerve to repair the gear lever for their own use afterwards. I didn't bother to confront them. They had their little victory, but in the end, it was I who got back in one piece, and that was all that mattered.

The Germans were housed in confined quarters but I was stationed in an old mansion house, a sprawling, majestic place that must have once belonged to the Lord of Appiano, or some other local aristocrat before the war swept it into the hands of the army. The mansion was the biggest house in the area, towering above everything else with an air of faded grandeur. A seven-foot-high stone wall enclosed the grounds, which stretched out for a good quarter-mile in each direction, the place had once been a fortress of luxury and privilege. It was a world away from the rough conditions of the front line where survival came first and comfort was a distant dream.

Within the walls, several warehouses stood—dark, looming structures built by the German or Italian armies, crammed with the spoils of war. Boots, shoes, clothes, all stolen from God knows where. The loot of a defeated enemy. Those warehouses were off-limits to us, locked up tight, but we knew what was inside. We'd heard the stories. Tempting as it was to break in and see for ourselves, no one dared. Orders were orders, even here.

The mansion itself housed about thirty of us British soldiers, with twelve crammed into each grand bedroom, which had once been the quarters of nobility, now filled with rough army bunks. But despite the crowded conditions, it was a good billet—far better than anything we'd had in the infantry. The food was plentiful, a welcome change from the meagre rations we were used to. Proper meals, hot and filling, not the tasteless, half-starved portions we had subsisted on while fighting at the front.

I was part of a group of twelve men in charge of distributing rations to the troops, a simple, steady job. We were in charge of issuing food and supplies, and had the help of two German soldiers. These were no hardened SS men; they were young, defeated, and willing to do whatever was asked of them. They were easy enough to get along with— men like us, soldiers trying to make sense of what was left after the war had chewed up so many lives and dreams.

All in all, life at the mansion was calm. It was a strange twilight existence, in a land still healing from war's devastation, surrounded by the remnants of another man's riches, waiting for orders that would take us to our next destination. But for the moment, we were safe, well-fed, and living in a place that still echoed with the past's grand ambitions, though now it housed nothing more than weary soldiers and stolen goods.

One afternoon, an American soldier turned up at our depot. He looked haggard, worn out, and somewhat desperate as he spoke to our officers, asking if he could stay with us until his own unit could come to collect him. I'd seen a fair few stragglers and lost men in my time, soldiers caught between the lines or separated from their companies, so this wasn't anything out of the ordinary. They gave him some food and a spare bunk in our large bedroom, where about twelve of us slept together in a cluttered, crowded space.

The Yankee had bandages wrapped around his arms and ankles, which he explained were from some accident in the mountains with his vehicle. His story didn't sound far-fetched, but there was something about the way he carried himself that made me uneasy. Maybe it was the way his eyes darted around the room, taking stock of everyone and everything. But we were soldiers, all of us, and trust didn't come easily.

That night, as we settled into our bunks, he climbed into the bed next to mine. I was drifting into that half-sleep soldiers get used to, always alert, when I saw him do something that snapped me awake. He slid his hand under his pillow and slipped a handgun beneath it. My instincts flared immediately. There was no reason for a man to sleep with a gun under his pillow in the middle of our own camp, surrounded by allies. It didn't sit right with me.

I turned to him my voice low but firm. "Why the gun under your pillow?" I asked, narrowing my eyes at him. "Put it in your bag, or you don't sleep near my bed. You go outside to sleep." I wasn't about to take any chances with a stranger armed in the night.

He looked at me for a moment, eyes flickering with something between surprise and reluctance. But he must've sensed I wasn't going to back down. Slowly, without a word, he reached under his pillow, pulled the handgun out, and shoved it into his small backpack. Only then did I feel the tension ease, but the suspicion lingered. Something about this man wasn't right, but at least for now, the gun was out of his hands.

We lay there in the darkness, the silence thick with unspoken wariness. I kept one eye open that night, just in case.

He was a friendly enough chap, that much I could say

for him. After a few days at the depot, the American soldier started tagging along with me and my mates whenever we went into the village for a drink. He could speak German fluently, which came in handy at the local inns. It was strange to have an American soldier mixing with us, but he seemed eager to be part of the group, and in a place like that, camaraderie was all we had.

One night, after we'd downed a few drinks and stepped out of the inn into the crisp mountain air, he did something that made my blood run cold. With a wild grin on his face, he pulled out that same handgun I'd seen him hide under his pillow. Before any of us could react, he raised it and started firing at the street lamps around the village square, shattering the bulbs with precision. One after another, they went out, leaving us in near darkness.

The others stood there, frozen, terrified of this sudden burst of madness. They weren't used to this kind of reckless behaviour, especially in a place where gunfire meant more than just noise. To them, it was a sign of danger, of death lurking close by. But I wasn't about to let him carry on. I stepped forward and grabbed his arm, forcing him to lower the gun.

"Cut it out," I said, my voice hard. "You do that again, and you're out of our camp. No exceptions."

He looked at me, his face still twisted in that cocky grin, but there was something behind his eyes—he knew I wasn't playing games. Slowly, almost begrudgingly, he holstered the gun. The others breathed a sigh of relief, but the tension still hung in the air, thick and heavy. He thought he could scare us, make us fall in line with his wild antics, but I wasn't having any of it.

That night marked a shift. He realized I wasn't someone to be pushed around, and after that, he clung to my company like a lost dog. Wherever I went, he wanted to come along. He even started talking about how I should visit him in Texas when all of this was over. Kept telling me we'd be great friends, like brothers in arms.

But I ignored him. There was something about the man I couldn't trust, a darkness that ran deeper than his friendly façade. He might've been playing the part of the jovial American soldier, but that gun told me a different story. And I knew better than to get too close to someone like that.

About a week later, he vanished without a word. I heard he'd gone to stay in one of the inns in the village, but I didn't care enough to ask where or why. Frankly, I was glad to see the back of him. He'd been a loose cannon, and I had no time for that kind of trouble, especially when we were still trying to keep some semblance of order in the wake of the war.

A week after he disappeared, two military police turned up. They were British, their uniforms crisp, eyes sharp as they sized me up. "You know this American soldier?" one of them asked, holding up a photo of the Yank.

I felt my blood rise. "He's no friend of mine," I shot back. "What's this about?"

They exchanged glances before one of them spoke. "We've arrested him. He's in prison now, up in Bolzano."

That took me by surprise. "What for?"

"Turns out your pal was an American deserter," the second MP said, his tone grim. "He belonged to a gang that's been stealing entire train wagons of food supplies and selling them on the black market in Austria. They've been running a racket for months, and we only just got a lead on them."

I stared at them, hardly believing what I was hearing. A deserter, running black market schemes out of war-torn Italy? It made sense in hindsight. The bandages, the suspicious behaviour, his strange need to carry that gun—he was hiding more than just his scars. The man had been living a double life right under our noses, and we hadn't even seen it.

"I told you, he was no friend of mine," I repeated, calmer this time. "I had no idea about any of this."

They nodded, clearly satisfied. "We've got what we need, then. Just wanted to confirm you weren't involved."

As they left, I stood there, still trying to wrap my head around it. The Yank had fooled us all, playing the part of the injured soldier while running criminal operations behind our backs. Now he was locked up in Bolzano, his schemes finally catching up with him.

It was a reminder, a sharp one, that in the chaos following the war, not all battles were fought on the front lines. Some men, like that Yank, would do anything to profit from the ruins. But justice had a way of finding them, one way or another.

While he was in our camp, apparently the Yank had noticed a stack of tyres piled against the back wall of the warehouse, half-hidden from view. To most, they were just old army supplies, gathering dust. But to him, they were an opportunity. He had a knack for sniffing out things that could be turned into profit. It wasn't long before he slipped back to Bolzano, where he'd already connected with a black-market gang operating in the shadows. It seemed he'd been plotting the whole thing from the moment he set foot in our camp.

He cut a deal with the gang, showing them where the tyres were stored and arranging for their lorry to come in the dead of night. When they arrived, he passed the tyres over the wall while his gang collected them. It was a smooth operation, and he was paid handsomely for it—millions of lire. While the rest of us were living off army rations and barely scraping by, he was living like a king in that small village inn, the one he disappeared to.

When the military police finally caught up with him, they found a suitcase stuffed with lire notes under his bed. The man had been living large, his greed finally betraying him. He was spending too much, too fast, and it didn't take long for word to spread through the local gossip mill. That's what tipped off the Military Police. They arrested him, suitcase and all, and put him behind bars.

But that wasn't the end of it. Rumour had it, the bandages he always kept wrapped around his arms and ankles were hiding more than just war wounds. Beneath those clean, white strips of fabric were ugly sores—the advanced stages of syphilis, eating away at him from the inside. He was rotting, even as he played the part of a wheeler-dealer, thinking he had the world in his hands.

The war may have ended, but the vultures were still circling, and some men, like that Yank, would do anything for a quick fortune, even if it destroyed them in the end.

With the episode of the Yank over we returned to normality but the duties of our Bulk Supply Depot were not confined to one area, we were sometimes moved on. The time came to prepare for a journey to Vienna in Austria, a city steeped in history and culture, nestled beyond the towering Italian Alps. The morning dawned crisp and clear, a golden sun rising over the jagged peaks, casting long shadows across the rugged terrain. Our convoy was set to leave early, the air thick with anticipation.

I was assigned to a small scout car, a nimble vehicle that would dart up and down the length of the convoy, ensuring all was secure as we made our way through the winding mountain passes. Bandits operated in the area and were known to pick off any straggling vehicles. The roar of engines filled the air, a mechanical symphony accompanied by the distant echo of birds taking flight.

As we climbed higher, the landscape transformed; lush valleys gave way to steep, rocky outcrops dusted with snow. The roads were treacherous, twisting sharply with steep drops on either side, but the beauty was undeniable. Every turn revealed breathtaking vistas, valleys sprawling below us like emerald carpets.

The convoy moved steadily, a string of vehicles, each carrying supplies crucial for our mission. I glanced back, watching as the trucks rumbled forward, laden with rations and gear for the troops waiting in Vienna. The soldiers were counting on us.

With each mile, I felt the thrill of adventure coursing through me. The mountains stood tall, guardians of secrets and stories yet to be uncovered. I was ready for whatever lay ahead in the grand city of Vienna, my spirit buoyed by the promise of new beginnings.

As we reached the summit and began our cautious traverse across the flat expanse, our scout car suddenly came to a halt. A sense of unease washed over me; one lorry from our convoy was conspicuously absent.

We retraced our route down the slope, and there, to our disbelief, was the driver—a foolhardy man—engaged in idle conversation with two young women. It was a scene ripe with danger, a perfect bait laid out by lurking road bandits, waiting for the last vehicle to wander into their grasp. The girls' laughter rang hollow against the backdrop of the mountains, a deceptive allure masking the peril that lay just beyond. We shouted, urgency crackling in our voices, but I could feel the tension coiling in the air, a warning that we were teetering on the edge of disaster. They could hear the anger in our voices and cut off their petty discussions to resume driving.

Climbing again to the summit, we resumed our route along the flat top, but soon encountered a fork in the road. Anxiety tightened in my gut as I scanned the horizon for a sign of our convoy. Standing atop the roof of the lorry, we peered into the distance, searching for any hint of direction, but the landscape offered no answers. Left or right? With no better choice, we took the left fork, hoping it would lead us back to the convoy.

We drove on for half a mile, the tyres crunching on gravel, when suddenly a small archway bridge loomed ahead. My heart raced as I noticed a sentry box on one side. Before we could react, two soldiers emerged, their machine guns raised and pointed directly at us. Russian soldiers, their expressions hard as flint, blocked our path, their intent clear.

We had veered onto the wrong road, and the realization settled like ice in my veins. The soldiers barked commands, their voices harsh and guttural as they shouted in Russian, gesturing for us to vacate the vehicle. There was a savage glint in their eyes, the threat of violence hanging palpably in the air. I felt the weight of my rifle, the instinct to defend ourselves battling with the wisdom of surrender. With my heart pounding, I exchanged glances with my comrades, knowing that this was a moment that could turn fatal in an instant.

With our hands raised high, we spoke in English, hoping against hope that these soldiers could see our mistake, that we bore no ill will. They herded us against the cold, unforgiving wall, their eyes narrowed with suspicion. We stood there, hearts pounding, for what felt like an eternity.

A Russian officer appeared, his presence commanding, as he gestured for us to follow him into the heart of his town. The streets, lined with barren buildings and the remnants of war, loomed before us like sentinels. All the while, the Russian soldiers clung to the doors of our vehicles, their machine guns pointed menacingly at us, the cold metal glinting ominously in the harsh light.

We moved under the watchful eyes of these soldiers, their faces hardened by conflict and suspicion. As we drove through the town, we caught fleeting glimpses of daily life interrupted by the spectre of military control—children playing in the shadows, wary glances exchanged, and the distant echoes of laughter stifled by the weight of authority.

In that moment, the reality of our predicament sank in; we were pawns in a game far beyond our understanding, caught in a world where alliances shifted like the winds that swept through the mountains. The officer led us deeper into the town, and I could feel my heart racing, knowing that our fate hung precariously in the balance.

We were all on edge, hearts pounding with uncertainty. Not one in our convoy knew where we had strayed, leaving them in the dark about our fate. In that grim moment, the reality struck us: these Russians could very well have kept us prisoners indefinitely.

We were ushered from our vehicles into what looked like the old town hall building. The Russian officer, a wiry little man with thick glasses perched on his nose, eyed us with a penetrating suspicion. He demanded to know who was the officer in charge, his voice laced with a mistrust that sent a chill down my spine. Were we deserters, or perhaps spies sent to inspect their treatment of the townspeople?

One by one, we were led away, the oppressive presence of a machine-gun-toting soldier shadowing our every step. The dimly lit corridor seemed to stretch endlessly, each creak of the floorboards echoing our anxiety. When my turn came, I found myself ushered into a bleak room, where the flickering light from a solitary bulb cast long shadows across the walls.

I was seated in a large chair, its size almost mocking in contrast to my mounting dread. The harsh light bore down on me, illuminating my face while obscuring everything else. In that moment, I felt like a prisoner under scrutiny as I prepared to face the interrogation that loomed ahead.

The Russian officer's voice echoed in the dim room, demanding answers. Though I couldn't see his face, the intensity of his presence loomed large, as if the very air was thick with his scrutiny. "Repeat what you said," he ordered, his tone cold and unyielding. "Why is there no officer with you?"

My heart raced. We had hurriedly rehearsed our story on the slow drive into town, an unbroken line of truth.

We knew the consequences of a slip—deserters or spies, the labels hung heavy in the air like a guillotine waiting to fall. We exchanged quick glances, silently reaffirming our resolve, and then I spoke, articulating the words we had memorized.

"The convoy was lost. A driver stopped for a chat, and we went back to find him." Each word was deliberate, a lifeline cast into the uncertain waters of our predicament. It was the truth, and we clung to it, hoping it would shield us from the ominous fate that loomed so near.

After what felt like an eternity, parched and weary from the hours spent in that oppressive room, the officer finally relented. "Get back into your vehicles," he commanded, his eyes still sharp, betraying no hint of the tension that had filled the air. A strange mix of relief and apprehension washed over us as we climbed back into our vehicles, Russian guards flanking us like sentinels, their machine guns glinting ominously in the fading light.

As we navigated the narrow streets, the moment weighed heavily, knowing how close we had come to a fate far worse than mere detention. Finally, we reached the spot where we had entered the town. The officer gestured sharply, his voice cold and unyielding: "Go fast. Before we change our minds."

We wasted no time. Tyres screeched as we sped away, hearts pounding in unison, a collective sigh of relief escaping our lips. The wrong turn had led us into a dark chapter, but now, as we regained the road that wound toward Vienna, we felt the taste of freedom return—bitter, sweet, and hard-earned.

Somehow, we managed to retrace our steps and locate

where our convoy had taken refuge. Arriving there, I was struck by an eerie calm; no one had even realized we were missing. The commanding officer, a grizzled man with eyes that had seen too much, listened to our tale with a mixture of disbelief and irritation. "You lot are lucky I don't put you on a charge for straying from the convoy," he barked, his voice echoing in the tense silence.

I couldn't shake the chill that coursed through me at the thought of what might have been—if the Russians had chosen to keep us as their own, we would have simply vanished, swallowed by the shadows of war.

I can't say how long we lingered in Vienna, that city steeped in history and charm. A few of us ventured into the sprawling Vienna Woods, the air fresh and invigorating, our spirits lifted by the sight of majestic trees draping over the trails. Horseback, we roamed through the emerald expanse, laughter echoing against the bark of ancient oaks.

Afterward, we made our way to the famed beer cellars, those cavernous spaces where the cool stone walls held secrets of ages past. The Austrian lager flowed like liquid gold, its flavour rich and robust, though the price reminded us we were no longer in the trenches. Each sip was a celebration, a toast to our survival and to the fleeting joys of life amidst the ruins of war. In that moment, surrounded by comrades and the warmth of camaraderie, I felt a flicker of hope that perhaps we could reclaim a semblance of normality, if only for a little while.

CHAPTER 20

KLAGENFURT: THE FINAL OUTPOST

A Tale of Brotherhood, Reflection, Rations and Regrets

O UR UNIT WAS ON THE move again, as the wheels of our convoy rolled into Klagenfurt, the crisp mountain air mingled with the lingering scent of war. This quaint town, nestled amidst the rugged beauty of Austria, became our sanctuary—a last refuge before the curtain fell on our tumultuous journey.

I found myself here at the age of 23 until the fateful day when I would finally be demobbed in February 1947. Five years had passed in a blur, three and a half of those spent on foreign soil, amidst the echoes of gunfire and the cries of the fallen. Klagenfurt was to be my final chapter, a bittersweet conclusion to a saga that had shaped me into the man I was today.

Every corner of this town whispered stories of resilience and survival, and as I moved through its streets, I couldn't help but reflect on the brothers I had lost and the bonds I had forged. In the shadow of the Alps, I felt a strange sense of peace wash over me, knowing that my time in this beautiful land was drawing to a close.

Klagenfurt lingers in the recesses of my mind, a tapestry woven from fleeting moments and long hours under a heavy sky. Each day, from the first light of dawn until the shadows stretched long in the evening, we toiled tirelessly, supplying rations to the units scattered across that rugged landscape.

The scent of earth and machinery hung in the air, punctuated by the distant rumble of trucks and the murmur of soldiers going about their daily grind. Each ration we issued bore the weight of our collective sacrifices—hard biscuits, dried beans, and precious lard, a commodity more valuable than gold in those desperate times.

Amidst the hustle and bustle, I often found myself lost in thought, reflecting on the camaraderie cast in the heat of duty. Klagenfurt, with its quaint charm and the spectre of war ever-present, became a backdrop to my journey—a place where the echoes of conflict met the resilience of the human spirit.

I occupied a modest room within a long imposing structure that lay in the heart of a dusty courtyard surrounded by the remnants of a world ravaged by war. Within these walls, I found myself sharing space with four German soldiers—men who had once been my enemies, now reduced to prisoners of war, yet tasked with labouring under my command.

Their presence was a constant reminder of the fragile

balance of power and the strange twists of fate that had brought us together. Each morning, as the sun broke over the horizon, we would gather in the courtyard, with the smell of fresh earth and the promise of another day of toil. These men, clad in tattered uniforms, looked to me for direction, their eyes reflecting a mix of resignation and a flicker of hope for a future beyond their confinement.

As we worked side by side, the barriers of language and ideology began to dissolve, revealing the shared humanity beneath our uniforms. They were no longer mere captives in my charge; they were men like me, bound by circumstance and yearning for an end to the madness that had engulfed us all. In that unlikely camaraderie, I found a kinship that transcended the labels of soldier and prisoner, a reminder that, in the end, we were all brothers in arms against the tides of war.

I held full responsibility for the contents of my store, a sprawling depot stocked with the lifeblood of every unit in the area—rations that were essential for survival, both in the field and at the base. Every day, trucks and lorries would rumble through the gates, their engines coughing to a halt as drivers waited for their share of supplies. Each vehicle required something different, its load determined by the size of the unit it was destined for, the needs of the men, and the demands of the terrain they were navigating.

It was a constant juggling act, ensuring the balance was maintained, that nothing was squandered or stolen. Flour, dried beans, tins of meat—every item mattered, and I made sure each unit got its due, no more and no less. The Germans who worked under me, prisoners of war, carried out the heavy lifting, under my watchful eye. There was no room for error, and I was ever vigilant, knowing that each ration I issued could be the difference between endurance and collapse, between strength and failure in the harsh post-war days of recovery.

In my store, lard and hard biscuits were the staple commodities, but lard—it was the real treasure. Like gold on the black market, it held a value that far surpassed its practical use. Every soldier, every local, knew its worth. A single tin of lard could be bartered for almost anything—cigarettes, clothes, even favours. Alongside it, we issued dried beans and peas, simple fare that kept the men nourished, though it lacked the allure of the precious lard.

Each day, as the vehicles lined up and the German POWs toiled under my supervision, I kept a close eye on the stock. I knew full well the temptation it presented. There wasn't a man alive who wouldn't risk a little thievery for a chance at the fortune a single container of lard could bring. But I ran a tight operation, and I wasn't about to let anything slip through unnoticed.

One afternoon, as the routine unfolded in the depot, I noticed one of the German prisoners struggling with a container of biscuits near the window. His movements were awkward, his arms trembling under the weight. Something wasn't right. I ordered him to halt. "Put it down," I barked, suspicion flaring inside me. He obeyed, the container thudding heavily onto the floor.

Curiosity, and years of instinct honed by survival in war, drove me to investigate. I bent down to lift it myself, and immediately, the weight was off—far too heavy for a box of biscuits. I pried it open, and there it was. The box was packed with lard—stolen piece by piece from the daily rations.

Fury welled up inside me. These men, these prisoners, had been siphoning off lard, bit by bit, saving it to sell on the black market. They'd been quietly building their fortune while the rest of us laboured to keep everything running smoothly. The audacity of it made my blood boil. In this war-scarred land, where food was life, they'd dared to turn necessity into profit.

They fell to pleading immediately, their faces pale with fear. "Please, Herr Sergeant," they begged, their voices thick with desperation. "We did not mean any harm. Don't report us. If you do, we'll be sent to prison for this. We cannot afford that. Not now, not after all that has happened."

I stood there, arms folded, my jaw clenched. There was no denying their guilt, but in that moment, I could see the bare truth—they were just men trying to survive, like all of us. War had turned the world upside down, and they were caught in its ruthless tide.

I took a long breath and made my decision. "Fine," I said, my voice steely, "I won't report you. But you'll return every scrap of lard you've stolen. A little at a time, added back to each ration."

Relief flooded their faces, though shame lingered in their eyes. I couldn't keep the lard stored in the depot—not with the rampant hunger and the black-market thriving—so piece by piece, we gave it back.

Otto, the one who spoke English the best, often handled the negotiations with the others. Despite the situation, we got along well, and gradually they came to respect my position. Otto in particular started looking up to me, his sharp eyes reflecting an unspoken bond. War made strange companions of us all, and though we stood on different sides, we all sought the same thing: survival.

Every morning, like clockwork, at the 10 o'clock break, one of the Germans—always punctual, always precise—would bring me a thick, juicy steak nestled between slices of fresh bread. The aroma of the cooked meat filled the air, a welcome reprieve from the dry, tasteless rations we were often used to.

I knew well where it came from—the Germans working in the butcher's store and the cookhouse, men who had once fed the soldiers of the Reich, now feeding me, their former enemy. It was an unspoken arrangement, one that reflected the strange new order we found ourselves in.

As I sat there, sinking my teeth into the soft bread and tender steak, I could almost forget the war for a moment. The taste of the meat, the quiet camaraderie that had developed between us—it was a reminder that, in the end, we were all just men, trying to get by in a world that had been turned upside down.

I came to realize, as the days passed, that the German soldier was no different from the British soldier. They were men cut from the same cloth—wearied by the same struggles, burdened by the same scars. In truth, you could say we were like brothers, united not by the uniforms we wore but by the shared weight of survival in a world that had gone mad.

These men, who once stood on the other side of the battlefield, didn't want the war any more than we did. It wasn't them who had plunged Europe into chaos, but Hitler and his fanatical Nazi movement, twisting the hearts of a nation. The soldiers I worked alongside weren't the monsters we'd been led to believe. They were fathers, sons, brothers, all caught in a storm not of their making, trying to find their way through the aftermath.

We had fought against each other in the name of duty, but here, in the quiet moments of our postwar existence, it was clear that neither of us had truly wanted the madness that had engulfed us. The real enemy had never been the man standing across the trench, but the forces of hate and power that had driven us all to the brink.

CHAPTER 21

ESCAPE FROM
THE ASHES

**In the aftermath of destruction,
the only way out is forward.**

A T LAST, THE MOMENT HAD come. After more than three long years abroad, I was granted a fortnight's leave—a fleeting taste of home. It was early 1946, and the war had left its scars on all of us, but the thought of seeing familiar faces again felt like a lifeline after all the chaos.

A couple of us piled into a military truck, our destination the train station in Villach, a large Austrian city and major traffic junction for southern Austria. Hundreds of soldiers were already there, eager to make the long trek through wartorn Europe and back to the shores of England. The train rattled through France, the countryside still bearing the marks of battle, until we finally reached the port of Calais.

From there, it was onto a small ship, a weather-beaten vessel carrying the promise of home.

But war has a way of lingering, even in those quiet moments between battles. As we sailed across the channel, a voice crackled over the Tannoy, echoing through the ship with a stern warning: "Any man found in possession of German or Italian handguns will be sent back to Austria and face prison."

The announcement sent a ripple through the crowd. You could feel the tension—no one wanted to risk missing their leave. Within minutes, the portholes became makeshift disposal units. Pistols, Lugers, and sidearms, all war trophies, were tossed into the sea by the dozens. I reckon there were over a hundred guns chucked into the cold waters of the Channel that day. Nobody cared about their souvenirs anymore. The thought of home—of a warm bed, a family meal, and a return to some semblance of normality—was worth more than any relic of the war.

We were soldiers desperate to shed the weight of the past, if only for a brief reprieve. The sight of the English coastline on the horizon was enough to make the whole ship buzz with life again. Everyone wanted to get home, even if it was only for a fortnight.

It was a strange, almost surreal moment, sitting on that tube train as it rattled beneath the streets of London. The hum of the city outside was familiar, yet distant, like a dream half-forgotten. Then, I heard it—a little girl chattering to her mother in English. After three long years of foreign tongues and broken phrases, the sound of my own language struck me like a bolt of lightning. It was so ordinary, yet in that moment, it felt profound. I hadn't realised just how much I'd missed the simple things, like the voices of home.

When I finally stepped into my old street, the world seemed to slow. There they were—my family, my neighbours, the people I'd grown up with, all standing at their front doors, their eyes wide with anticipation. Someone must have seen me coming from the station, and word had spread like wildfire. It was as if the entire street had come to a standstill, waiting for my return.

And then I saw her. My mother, standing a few houses down, her hands covering her mouth in disbelief. The moment she recognized me, she burst into a sprint, running up the street with her arms wide open, her face a mix of joy and tears.

It was more than just a homecoming—it was a reminder of everything I'd fought for, everything we'd all endured. My mother reached me first, throwing her arms around me, and in that embrace, the weight of the past three years seemed to fall away. I was home. Finally, I was home.

The fortnight passed in a blur, and I have to admit, it was dull. After all the excitement of coming home, reality set in soon enough. My old friends, the blokes I used to share drinks and stories with, were still away in the forces, scattered across Europe and beyond. The streets of Wales felt strangely empty, hollow even. The war had touched everything, and though it was over, the wounds were still fresh.

I found myself restless, pacing through days that stretched out long and slow. Even the food was a constant reminder of the hardships. Rationing was still in full force— meagre portions of bread, butter, meat doled out carefully.

It was nothing like what I'd grown used to back in Austria, where our depot was well-stocked, and I could eat my fill without thinking twice.

So, in a strange way, I was almost relieved when it came time to head back. Austria, for all its scars, had become a place of routine, of purpose. I longed for the work again, to be surrounded by men who understood the strange limbo we all found ourselves in after the war had ended but before life had truly begun again.

Eventually, my time came. Demobbed at last. When we arrived at Folkestone, they herded us into a vast, echoing shed, a place that felt as impersonal as the barracks we'd left behind. Inside, rows of counters stretched out, manned by men who barely lifted their heads as we approached. It was like stepping into some strange market, but instead of rations or army supplies, they handed out shirts, ties, suits—civilian clothes, stacked neatly like they belonged to another life.

There was a surreal moment, standing in line, trading my uniform for a suit and tie. It felt like shedding a skin, leaving behind the soldier I had been for so long. The transformation happened quickly, almost too quickly. We went in soldiers—men who had seen the harshness of war, who had lived in foreign lands under foreign skies—and we came out the other side, dressed like ordinary civilians. But beneath the new fabric, I knew nothing about me had changed. War had shaped us in ways that no suit could cover up.

Walking out of that shed, I wasn't sure if I felt relief or something closer to loss. The world expected us to return to normal, to slip back into the rhythm of peacetime as if the war had never happened. But deep down, I knew that part of me would always belong to those years spent under the sun and snow of foreign battlefields.

The soldier was gone, but the war would stay with me forever.

I had over three months of leave stacked up, earned one day for every month spent abroad. It was a strange feeling, to have so much time handed to me, after years of marching to the relentless beat of orders and duty. But I had a plan, a clear intention that kept me focused amidst the haze of returning home.

South Africa called to me. Not the war-torn Europe I had left behind, but a land vast and untamed, where opportunity seemed to hang in the air like the scent of wild earth. The government was launching a scheme to produce oil from groundnuts—peanuts, harvested by the natives, while we would oversee the operation. It seemed like the perfect venture, something that combined adventure with a sense of purpose, of rebuilding after the destruction I had witnessed.

The promise of the African sun, of wide-open lands and the challenge of shaping a new enterprise, stirred something inside me. The war might have ended, but there was a new frontier on the horizon, one that I was eager to conquer. The groundnut scheme—it sounded practical, yet it held the allure of something greater. We would be part of the next wave, the men who helped build an empire not with bullets, but with the soil beneath our feet.

South Africa wasn't just a place; it was the future. A chance to leave behind the grey, rationed existence of post-war Britain and forge something new. The thought of supervising the native labour, of working under the fierce African sun, felt like a natural extension of everything I had learned in the military. Discipline, leadership, survival—it was all the same, but now applied to a new kind of battle: the battle to shape the land, to create wealth from the earth.

Howard Evans, my old friend from Marks and Spencer, had caught the glint of adventure in my eye when I first spoke about the South African groundnut scheme. He'd seemed keen at the start, nodding along as I spun tales of wide, sun-baked lands and the opportunity to shape something with our bare hands. "I'll come with you," he'd said, the excitement in his voice unmistakable. It was enough for me to hold back from applying straight away, to wait for him to make his move.

But two months passed, and the fire in Howard's belly had all but fizzled out. Slowly, I began to see the truth—he wasn't going. He'd returned to his familiar life in Cardiff, slipping back into the routine of Marks and Spencer, as if the war, the call of Africa, had never existed. The wild frontier I'd imagined no longer held the same appeal to him, and before long, I realized he'd simply settled for the quiet hum of everyday life.

And so had I. The more I delayed, the more distant South Africa seemed. Before I knew it, I was back at Marks and Spencer myself, slipping into the old groove like a pair of worn shoes, fitting back into the life I had known before I was called up. The rhythm of it—stocking shelves, tallying orders, the everyday banter with colleagues—felt like a strange comfort, a return to normality after the chaos of war.

But deep down, a part of me bristled at the routine. There had been a moment when the world had felt wide open, full of possibilities, and now here I was, back where I had started, feeling the weight of missed chances settling on my shoulders.

It must have been fate, pure and simple, when I first laid eyes on the redheaded girl in the staff department. There was something about her that stirred a spark in me, something fierce and untouchable in her eyes, unlike anyone I'd ever known. She wasn't like the other girls who easily said yes when I asked them out. No, she always turned me down with a smile, but somehow that only made me want her more. I couldn't quite shake her from my thoughts, and in those moments between stacking shelves and tallying up stock, I found myself wondering what it was about her that held my interest so fiercely.

But work indoors, boxed in by the four walls of the shop, was stifling. I felt like a caged lion, restless and eager to break free. I knew, deep down, that it wasn't for me. Eventually, I reached my limit. Leaving Marks and Spencer behind, I took an outdoor job on the railway at Cathays Yard. I figured the open air, the clanging of trains, and the bustle of men hard at work would satisfy that gnawing need for something more.

It didn't.

No matter how much I tried to convince myself otherwise, it wasn't the life I wanted. Standing on the tracks, with the cold wind whipping through the yard, I realized it wasn't enough to be outdoors—I still wanted adventure, the thrill of the unknown. My heart yearned for the wild, untamed lands beyond Britain's shores. I thought about

South Africa, about the government's ground nut scheme, but that dream had already died—closed up just as I had been ready to leap. The chance was gone.

And so, I was stuck in Cardiff, my dreams of adventure slipping further out of reach with each passing day. The world had moved on, but the fire in my chest still burned, seeking something I couldn't quite name.

A miracle, it seems, intervened to shield me from the horrific carnage at Salerno. In the heart of the chaos on the front line in Italy, I found myself inexplicably protected. First, a sniper's bullet struck my helmet, the impact rattling my very soul — a mere inch closer, and it would have pierced my skull, sealing my fate. Then came the merciless machine gun fire, bullets whipping past me as I sat outside my mate's pit, each crack a reminder of the danger that surrounded us.

The enemy was ruthless, a German soldier firing down upon us from his elevated position. Just as it seemed the tide was turning against us; fate played its hand. A hand grenade hurled by our brave Lance Corporal found its mark, and in a blinding flash, the German was silenced, his threat extinguished in an instant.

But the most profound moment came later. After I was pulled back from the line for a precious forty-eight hours of rest, I thought I saw Our Lady. In that fleeting vision, amidst the horror and grime of war, I felt an overwhelming sense of peace. It was as if she had come to reassure me that I was not alone, that some force beyond my comprehension was watching over me in this theatre of death. In that moment, I understood that I had been saved for a reason, spared from the abyss that claimed so many around me.

A lot of my mates never made it back when our company

pushed across that damned bridge. It was a massacre, a brutal crossing that claimed too many good men, friends I'd fought beside for months. But I wasn't with them. Fate, or something more elusive, had other plans for me. That detour, that one moment of hesitation, placed me far enough away from the front when the others went over the bridge. I should have been with them. I was supposed to be there. But I wasn't.

I had been sent back to camp that day, a dull ache in my knee that had steadily worsened until I could barely walk without wincing. The Medical Officer had no sympathy, of course. "You'll be back in the front line in no time," he'd barked at me, his hands prodding my knee like I was a stubborn piece of machinery. He didn't care that every step felt like a bayonet stabbing through the joint. To him, pain was a luxury no soldier could afford, and I was shoved back towards the front.

Yet, despite his orders, something pulled me toward the first aid post. I didn't even question it at the time. My leg was screaming at me with every step, and it felt like I had no choice but to seek relief, just for a moment.

Standing at the edge of the aid post, listening to the dull thud of artillery and the crack of rifle fire not far away, I knew that something more than just luck had steered me here. It was as though I had been plucked from the jaws of death at the very last moment. Even in the haze of war, with chaos swirling around me, I could feel it — a force greater than myself had kept me from crossing that bridge and would keep me safe again.

From then on, I found myself being sent further and further away from the front lines, like a leaf caught in a current, drifting with a purpose beyond my understanding. I was moved back through Italy, across the Mediterranean, until I reached the sprawling bustle of Algiers. By then, the war was far behind me, but the sense of survival, of some invisible hand guiding me, remained as sharp as ever. I knew, without a doubt, that I had been protected, spared from the violence for a reason. That reason became clear to me the day I met Hilda Morgan, the redhead from Marks and Spencer.

She needed my protection, and after she finally agreed to go out with me, together we carved out a life that felt divinely orchestrated. It wasn't just chance that brought us together; it was something greater—God's design, if you will. Together we built a loving Catholic family, the kind I believe the Almighty had intended for us. It was as though He had set the task before us, gifting us the love, the strength, and the will to face whatever hardships came our way.

That chapter of my life is one of immense love and challenge, but I won't delve into it further here. It was a journey as difficult as it was rewarding, full of struggles familiar to so many others in those post-war years. We were promised "Britain, a land fit for heroes." Codswallop! No one had money back then, not a penny to spare. If you wanted to survive, you had to work yourself to the bone, and that's exactly what we did. The dream we'd fought for during the war was no more than a hollow promise, a cruel irony for men who had given everything. But we carried on, Hilda and I, with faith and fortitude, as was demanded of us.

The four brothers returned home from the war, their faces weathered by the horrors they had witnessed, but their hearts still beating with the fierce pulse of survival. The world had changed, yet in some ways, it had stayed the same. They came back to the land they had fought for, their Welsh roots firmly planted in the soil of a country they had sworn to protect.

John, the eldest, married soon after his return. They had three children, each a reminder of the future they had all fought to secure.

Tom, the second brother, followed the same path, finding a partner to share his days. His own three children grew up under the shadow of the war, but their laughter filled the air, a testament to the resilience of the human spirit.

Danny, the third brother, never allowed his pain to keep him from building a life of his own. He married and had five children, each one a piece of his legacy, carrying with them the strength and memories of their father's struggles.

But it was Billy, the youngest, who would carry the weight of the past most profoundly. He married Hilda, the beautiful redhead from Marks and Spencer. She was a woman of fierce loyalty and love. Together, they built a family of their own, four children who would go on to have eleven grandchildren, their numbers swelling to thirteen great-grandchildren as the years passed. The family grew and prospered, as families do, but they never forgot the sacrifices made by those who came before them. The stories of the war, of courage and of loss, became the lifeblood of their gatherings, legendary tales passed down like a torch to the next generations.

As the years wore on, Billy, now an old man, felt the weight of his memories grow heavier still. In his eighties, he made a decision that would ensure the sacrifices of his comrades were never forgotten. He took pen to paper and recorded his memories, raw and unflinching, a testament to the suffering endured by these brave soldiers, whose lives were shaped by the brutal force of war. Through his words, the past came alive again, as if those who had been lost to time were still with them.

Billy lived a long and full life, reaching the grand age of 88. His journey took him to the gates of Buckingham Palace, where, in the twilight of his years, he was invited to meet Her Majesty the Queen at a veterans' garden party. It was a moment of recognition, not just for him, but for every soldier who had stood beside him, whose names were etched into the annals of history, but whose faces the world had long since forgotten.

In that moment, Billy stood tall—a living bridge between the past and the present—knowing that, through his words, their story would endure for generations to come.

18 years old 1940